How to Make Incredible Money in Technology $ales

How to Make Incredible Money in Technology $ales

Mike Slattery

ISBN-13: 9781721677818
ISBN-10: 172167781X

Table of Contents

Summary

I f you simplify it, there are only two core components to making incredible money in technology sales. Those two core components are generating more pipeline and closing more pipeline. That's it. I'm not going to tell you that you need more pipeline and you need to close more deals. You already know that. I'm going to show you the most efficient process for generating more pipeline and closing more deals, which will ultimately help you make incredible money in technology sales.

My commitment to you: I promise that if you read this book and implement these processes, you will save yourself time and increase your sales. If you're trying to break into technology sales, discuss these processes during the interview, and you will land a job at the right technology company. As they say, once is chance, twice is coincidence, and the third time is a pattern.

The sales processes in this book are what I have used to sell over one hundred net new logos, and I have never once missed a presidents club in my career. If you apply this system to your sales territory, you'll make more money and elevate your technology sales career.

I've conducted roughly one thousand discovery meetings. I've sold to CEOs of emerging technology companies, chief information officers

(CIOs) of Fortune 500 companies, CMOs of global brands, and chief supply chain officers (CSCOs) from blue-chip companies. This book and the integrated how-to videos will show you the detailed actions you need to take to be successful in technology sales year over year.

Regarding the first component of generating more pipeline, I'll show you how to stay motivated by fueling your resiliency fire. We'll lay a solid foundation by showing you the most efficient white-spacing process. Once we lay the foundation, we'll build you a core system of automation for driving new pipeline. We'll discuss a personalized messaging strategy that will drive new meetings with a click of a button. I'll show you how to break into any account with prospect journey mapping, and I'll show you how to leverage digital tools in the digital era to get a meeting with anybody.

Once we build your core system of automation to generate new pipeline, we will shift gears and focus on the second component of closing more pipeline. I'll show you how to master the discovery meeting. We'll discuss how to prepare and how to get the information you need to move the sale forward; even when you don't have access to the chief financial officer (CFO). I'll show you how to create internal champions via personal value to get the deal done. We'll discuss closing the sale with justification statements and how to stay top of mind between interactions.

Also, I'll provide value between those two core components, such as how to ensure your long-term sales success and stay ahead of your peers. I'll discuss the importance of becoming an agile sales professional and adapting to your new environment.

Most sales professional have ADD, so I've tried to keep this book as short as possible. Your time is valuable, and you don't want to waste your time. If you invest the time to apply the concepts in this book, you'll make more money.

Introduction

Early in my career, I started to follow the money and soon found that top technology salespeople are paid more than doctors, lawyers, and some C-level executives. Many of these salespeople were making $200,000 plus year over year with less than three years of professional selling experience. The great technology sales professionals are constantly pulling in $400,000 plus year over year. There are some in the perfect storm environment that can even make $1 million plus per year.

I want to set something straight about money: making money is not a bad thing. In fact, if you have money, one could argue you can do more for your community, such as donating to charity or local schools. You can absolutely become a multimillionaire in technology sales. You don't have to be the founder of your own company or become the CEO. I'm talking about becoming a millionaire as an individual contributor. All you need is a proven, consistent, disciplined sales process. If you do this right, you can constantly make $250,000 per year. Then play your cards right by investing a portion of that income. Finally, you need time to let your money grow. It's that simple. I am not a financial expert, nor is this book about financial guidance. This book is going to focus on the most important part of the equation, which is how to make incredible money in technology sales.

Why Was This Book Written?

There are thousands of sales books on the market. Many of these books discuss high-level theories about the right sales process and methodologies. Many of these books lack the details you need to know to make a ton of money. This book isn't going to discuss another high-level theory about B2B selling. This book was written by someone who is in the trenches right next to you.

I'm not going to tell you that you need more pipeline to generate more sales. Instead, we're going to discuss the detailed ACTIONS you need to take to generate more pipeline and ultimately be successful in the B2B technology world. This book is about taking action and ultimately helping you make incredible money in technology sales.

In this book, I'm going to share what I've learned throughout my technology sales career. This book is not about sales leadership strategies. This book is for the individual contributor who wants to earn as much money as he or she possibly can. But if you're a sales leader, helping your reps sell more will ultimately benefit you, so there is value here for you as well. We'll discuss the set of actions you need to take in your territory to be successful, and, most importantly, we'll discuss how to make incredible money in technology sales.

CHAPTER 1

Fueling the Resiliency Fire

I f you're going to succeed in professional technology selling, you will need to be confident, driven, and, most importantly, resilient. Before we discuss any sales tactic or sales process, we need to get your mind right. You must become mentally tough and confident and find the fuel that is going to make you the most resilient SOB anyone has ever met.

There is a saying in America's pastime (baseball) that great hitters fail seven out of every ten at-bats, thus giving them a .300 batting average. Think about that—the best players in the world fail much more than they succeed. Alternatively, think about the runner. Anyone who has ever run more than five miles knows that running long distances is much more about mental toughness than is it physical. The same is true for all great sales professionals; you will face more rejection than any other profession. The key is keeping the drive going and staying resilient throughout the course of your sales career.

When you wake up in the morning, you need to know you're the best or that you will become the best. Start telling yourself there is zero chance of any of your peers beating you ever! If you truly want to achieve greatness and reap all the financial rewards, you need to start by getting your mind right. I want you to keep telling yourself you're the best every single day for the next ninety days. If you tell yourself this long enough, you'll start believing it. Moreover, when you believe it, you can fully commit to making it happen no matter what obstacles you may face.

The more you start believing in yourself, the greater your confidence and conviction will become. People buy from sales professionals who show unwavering confidence and conviction in the value they provide. You must truly believe in yourself to produce the confidence that will make you great.

You're reading this book because you want to make more money or become better at professional selling. The question is, why do you want to make more money? In other words, what is the fuel for your fire? Is it to buy freedom? To pay for college, a better lifestyle, better health care, a better life for your kids? Whatever the reason is, don't forget it. Make up your mind right now—you're the best, and there is not a single person on this planet who is better than you. Now take that fire (whatever it is) and write it down somewhere in your home where you will see it every single day.

Tech sales is the greatest profession in the world. You can make $400,000 per year without enduring the risk of starting your own business or without managing any people. However, nothing worth having comes easy. If you want to make life-changing money, you must first become mentally tough.

How to Fuel Your Resiliency Fire

Resiliency is the ultimate trait of great salespeople. Sales professionals take the word "no" for a living, which can be hard at times. We need clear and concise goals to help add fuel to the resiliency fire.

If you're going to stay driven, you must first figure out the WHY behind wanting to make a ton of money. Then you need to set a timeline for when you want to stop working. I don't like the word *retirement;*

it makes me think of old people in Florida. I prefer to call it your *stop working point* because you'll have the luxury of enough time to do whatever you want.

As you get older, you realize time is much more valuable than money. However, money can ultimately buy you the luxury of spending time the way you want to. Understanding the WHY behind your long-term goals will help you stay driven over time.

If you want to be successful in professional selling, you must become resilient. If you want to be resilient, you need to self-reflect about what you want in the next ten years. You must truly understand why you want to make an incredible amount of money.

Setting short-term and long-term financial goals is the foundation for ensuring your long-term success in professional selling. For this exercise, we're going to use my buddy Cane as an example. Cane is thirty and married with three kids on one income, and he currently has $80,000 saved in his 401K.

Cane wants financial freedom for himself and his family. He wants to save enough money so he can live off the interest of his investments. Furthermore, he wants to stop working in fifteen years. His stop-working number is $2 million, but why $2 million? Cane knows that he only needs $10,000 per month to live a great life. Assuming 8 percent interest, Cane could withdraw $10,000 per month for thirty years and still have a retirement balance of $1.6 million to pass on to his family after thirty years.

(Use this calculator for this exercise)

So we now know the why behind the $2 million. How do we make this number achievable? Cane sets the end goal and reverse engineers the rest—Cane's decade or ten-year goal to become a millionaire. He has $80,000 in savings, and based on his comfortable lifestyle, he needs to save $4,600 per month, or $55,200 annually, to reach this goal. I get it—$55,200 per year in savings alone may seem like a ridiculous goal.

But we're in technology sales, and the sky's the limit. I'll show you how we make this achievable.

Cane's Ten-Year Goal

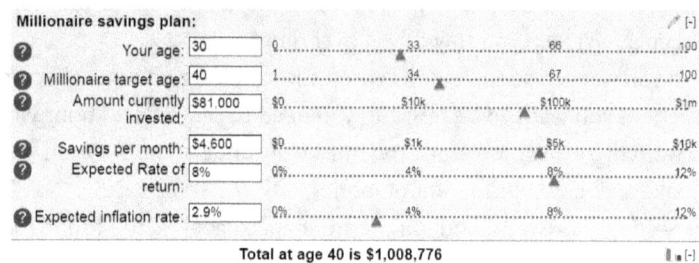

Total at age 40 is $1,008,776

Cane's Fifteen-Year Goal

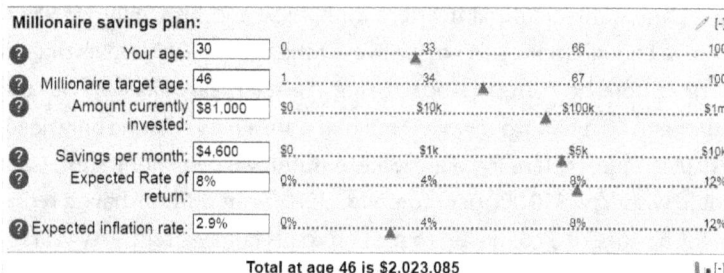

Total at age 46 is $2,023,085

How to Make any Goal Achievable by Breaking It Down

Cane knows the importance of setting long-term income goals. He knows that every year, he needs to contribute $55,200 to stay on track. Cane isn't one of those frugal people, either; he wants it all. He wants a great retirement starting at age forty-six, but he wants to take his family on great vacations and own a nice car. Cane looks at his annual expenses and decides how much money he needs to make year over year to accomplish these goals. He needs to earn $210,000 per year.

There will be days where you don't want to make that last cold call, the last meeting, or the last email. The most successful sales professionals find ways to stay motivated year over year. The best way to stay motived is to define your goals, which will add to your resiliency fire.

Cane's income goal is $210,000 gross per year. He works as a technology account executive selling human capital management software (HCM). His pay structure is the industry standard at 50/50, 50 percent base and 50 percent commission. His on-target earnings (OTE) are $210,000 per year, which means he is guaranteed $105,000 base, and he'll receive the other $105,000 for reaching his quota. His annual quota is $1 million.

His average deal is $100,000, and he averages about 10 percent commission on each deal. This equals about $10,000 in commission for each deal closed. At the beginning of each year, Cane analyzes the average deal size and understands that his discovery-call close ratio is about 5:1. This means for every five discovery meetings he books, he closes one deal on average.

At an average deal of $100,000, he'll need to close ten deals this year to achieve his income goal of $210,000 per year. He knows that with a discovery-to-close ratio of 5:1, he'll need to book about fifty discovery meetings this year to be successful.

$100,000 average deal size (X) 10 deals = quota achieved, or $105,000 in commission.

50 discovery meetings (5:1 will close). 50/5 = 10 deals needed.

Now you're starting to see that the monumental savings goal of $4,600 is starting to become more achievable as we further break down the goals. Cane now knows he needs to book fifty discovery meetings with an average size deal of $100,000 per year, or basically one discovery per week (50 discoveries/52 weeks = 1.04). As you're starting to see, we started with a big goal. The further we break it down, the more achievable our goal starts to become.

So, the real question: How much outbound activity does it take to achieve 1.04 discoveries per week?

Cane uses a multichannel approach (LinkedIn, direct mail, cold call, email, mail merge). He knows on average it takes about fifty outreaches to acquire one discovery meeting.

50 outreaches = 1 discovery meeting.

Cane needs 1.04 discoveries per week to stay on track. Thus, Cane's monthly activity goal needs to be at least two hundred outreaches per month, or fifty per week, or ten per workday.

Remember when you almost stopped reading this book because $2 million in savings seemed like a completely unachievable goal? Well, through this exercise, we've uncovered that on average, you need only about ten outreaches per day to achieve this goal. The numbers will change depending on a variety of factors, but the key point is that we just made an audacious goal achievable over time.

Blocking Out the Noise

The way most of the compensation plans are structured, you have 365 days a year to hit your annual quota. Most companies will have accelerators once you achieve your annual plan. This means you make more on every deal you sell once you hit your quota. At the end of the year, you'll go back to zero, and it starts all over again. This means that time is your biggest liability—you have 365 days to overachieve your quota, so spend your time doing activities that make you money.

Sounds simple, right? In the beginning, you'll need training to get up to speed. At some point, I want you to get comfortable with using the word "no," especially after you start to experience success. Don't get me wrong; it's very flattering when people value your experience and ask for your time. If you do too much of it, you will not achieve your financial objectives. You must shut off the noise and become a master of focus. Focus your energy on revenue-generating activities.

Shut off all negativity as well. After all, you're the best, and you've mentally committed that no one will beat you. Cut the cord on all negativity. Block out anyone and everything that is wasting your time.

CHAPTER 2

Chief Marketing Officer (CMO) and
Professional Sales—Building a System
of Core Automation

G ood salespeople make good money. Great salespeople make life-changing money. What makes some salespeople go from good to great? Do they work harder? Do they have more experience? The answer: maybe or maybe not.

We've all seen it. There is a handful of sales professionals at every company who seem to crush it every single year. Management is constantly trying to figure out what these people are doing differently to drive such great results. These high-performing reps have discipline, they're motivated, and they consistently do the right activities that drive results.

I believe these people work in two modes of operation:

1. CMO mode. This is the mode in which the reps are consistently educating and providing value to everyone in their territory, every single week. They approach their nonactive sales cycles as a CMO would. They know it's only a matter of time before they get a meeting, but they must consistently find ways to educate their market on the potential value they can deliver.

2. Professional sales mode. This is everything else. The point from where they get the first meeting with their prospect to the moment they close.

The greatest sales professionals—I'm talking about the professionals who make $250,000 to over $1 million year over year—have two modes of operation. They establish a solid foundation of contacts via data scrubbing and prioritizing accounts. Once they set up their database, they leverage personalized automation to drive new meetings consistently. This allows them to spend more time in professional sales mode and ultimately close more business.

Think about it: Ever wonder why there is always that person who seems to have a deal in play? It's because that person has two modes of operation. The main takeaway is to think strategically about how you're going to consistently educate your market. There will be several weeks where you get very busy.

The key is to develop a system that allows you to drive high activity even when you're slammed with other activities. If you don't do this, you'll see dips in your production down the road. With a six-month sales cycle average, what you do today will dictate your income six months from now.

If we can automate CMO mode, we'll have more consistent meetings, which equals more consistent pipeline, which equals more closed deals consistently—which ultimately equals more consistent income.

I'm going to show you a system that will automate your CMO mode to drive meetings so that you can spend more time in professional sales mode. I've always found that getting the discovery meeting is the hardest part of any sale. This system's core focus is about getting you more discovery meetings with qualified opportunities. To achieve more discovery meetings, we must lay a solid foundation, and this all starts with the most efficient data-scrubbing process.

The Foundation for Success: The Most Efficient Data-Scrubbing and White-Spacing Process

White spacing defined – The process of identifying and prioritizing prospects within your sales territory. Data scrubbing defined – The process of ensuring you have the correct data for your prospects. Data refers to the correct email address, phone number, job title, and other contact attributes. Nobody woke up and said, "I can't wait to start scrubbing data, finding emails and phone numbers, and white spacing my market." This process is painful but extremely important. Time is your biggest liability, as you have 365 days to hit a number, so you must spend your time with prospects that are going to give you the best chance to win.

You'll need some platform to manage your sales territory. If you're already working for a tech company, you'll most likely have a customer relationship management system (CRM) such as Salesforce. If you don't have Salesforce, that's OK. I'm going to show you how to manage your sales territory and execute personalized campaigns with Microsoft Office. Even if you have Salesforce, you'll still want to implement this system with Outlook.

I cannot stress this enough: if you do not spend the time to lay a solid foundation and scrub your territory's market, it will be extremely difficult for you to be successful. Don't assume your territory has clean or updated contact data, either. Bad data into your CRM equals bad data out. Even if you have a CRM like Salesforce, you cannot assume the contacts are clean and up to date. Take the time to scrub through the data. The other major benefit of doing this yourself is that this exercise will help you learn your territory inside and out.

Anytime I've ever started in a new sales territory, I've taken two weeks to scrub data, analyze, and prioritize my accounts. Now you should shake the trees if you're new to a role, which means run with any previous sales cycles that the rep before you might have had. However, I promise you if you follow my system, you will make more money and have more free time as a result of automation. When I say automation, I mean personalized messaging to every single contact in your territory with a click of a button. To achieve this, you need to lay a solid foundation by ensuring you identify any potential prospects in your territory.

Data Scrubbing Introduction

I'm going to show you the most efficient way to white space your entire territory. This process is systematically designed for efficiency, so it's important that you follow the order described below.

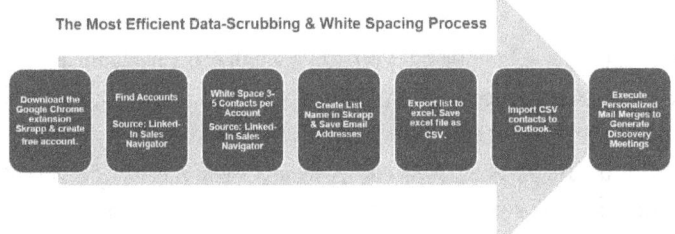

The Most Efficient Data-Scrubbing & White Spacing Process

Video - The Most Efficient Data-Scrubbing & White Spacing Process (Refer to e-book for video link)

Sales tools that are worth the cost and must-haves:

Use Google Chrome as your browser. We're going to download Chrome extensions for white spacing; click here.

ZoomInfo is the best source for email addresses. However, your company will need a formal relationship for you to get access. At the time of this writing, Zoom caters only to the large enterprise market for its customers. If you have access to ZoomInfo, download the ReachOut extension here.

Skrapp (Refer to e-book for the link to Skrapp) is the next-best free resource for email addresses. You get 120 email exports for free; then their paid accounts are very reasonable. Skrapp integrates directly with LinkedIn Sales Navigator. This will give you the ability to save email addresses directly from LinkedIn. Then I'll show you how to export the list and save it to your Outlook for executing personalized mail merges.

Microsoft Office—managing business and time, and prospecting automation.
LinkedIn Sales Navigator—white spacing.
Webex—meetings and nurturing sale cycles.
Yesware—email tracking and condensing content.

When you go live in your sales territory, you'll most likely be assigned a territory based on geo, vertical, revenue, annual spending, and named accounts. Let's say you're selling supply chain software with a focus on the health-care vertical. Your company gives you a list of one hundred accounts and says get it done. If you're building a list from scratch, I'll show you how to do this with tools such as LinkedIn Sales Navigator.

Your technology offering and value proposition will dedicate whom you want to target. When people think of technology decision makers, they traditionally think of targeting the CIO. This tends to be the case the majority of the time. However, every C-level executive needs to get his or her pulse on the technology landscape. Case in point: the CMO must now be a digital marketing technology expert. There are thousands of different MarCom technologies on the market.

When you start selling six-figure technology offerings, you'll have to navigate complex consensus buying that spans multiple departments and multiple stakeholders. Ideally, it's always best to start with power and work your way down. I recommended white spacing three to five contacts for each account.

Data Scrubbing—Step 1

Start by getting your list of target accounts and prospects in Sales Navigator. By now, you should have the ZoomInfo ReachOut extension or Skrapp installed from the Google Chrome store. You'll see the icons in the top right corner of your browser once either one is installed.

Both of these Chrome extensions integrate directly with LinkedIn. It will save you a massive amount of time by allowing you to pull the email addresses directly from your prospects' LinkedIn pages. Refer back to the most efficient data-scrubbing process video for additional instructions.

ZoomInfo, ReachOut, and Skrapp extensions (upper right-hand corner of your browser):

Why You Should Use Outlook to Manage Your Contacts, and How to Segment Your Outlook Database to Drive Personalized Automation

If you organize your contacts in the right way, you can send mail merges that look personalized. As you know, email has spam filters. As humans, we have spam filters as well. It takes us less than one-tenth of a second to know if someone sent us a personalized email or if we were part of a mass email. The trick is to use mass email in a way that is still personalized so that your prospect cannot tell the difference. Also, you want to provide value in the content of the email. If you provide value, prospects will be OK with you emailing them.

Implementing this system is critical to your long-term success. With this system, I can reach out to every single contact in my territory with a click of a button. When I'm busy traveling to meetings with prospects, my production never slips because I use personalized automation at scale to drive high activity.

Establishing this Outlook database will save you a tremendous amount of time in the future and allow you to book discovery meetings and nurture accounts with a click of a button.

How to Convert Contacts from Excel to Outlook
Video—How to Import a CSV File into Outlook and Segment your Sales Territory (Refer to e-book for video link)

Surprisingly, many salespeople I meet are still managing their contacts out of Excel. To be clear, I'm not telling you to abandon your CRM system. The challenge with many of these systems is the ability to deliver personalized mail merges at scale. If your current CRM system is booking meetings for you, then you can stop reading this portion.

If you want more meetings, more deals, and more commission, then this portion is critical to your success. Almost every CRM has an Export to Excel function. If all your territory contacts are in your CRM, find the Export to Excel function and then save that file. Finally, watch the ten-minute video above to upload your contacts correctly into Microsoft Outlook.

The Most Effective Way to Segment Your Sales Territory

Now that you have a solid foundation of contacts in Outlook, let's discuss the most effective way to tier and segment your sales territory.

On the left-hand column, you'll notice I've segmented my territory by the following:

Active Sales Cycles. Accounts that are currently in a sales cycle.

Pending Discoveries. Someone who has agreed to a meeting but is still not on the calendar.

Lead-Nurturing Accounts. Accounts that have said no. The way I see it, no is a temporary answer; we still need to provide value and have interactions with these contacts.

Core Prospects. Most companies sell multiple technology solutions. It's always easier to sell to an existing client than it is to a pure net new logo. Do your research and know if the prospect's company already has a relationship with your organization. For example, you work at Salesforce. Your prospect uses your CRM system, but you're selling the marketing cloud offering to the CMO. Leverage existing relationships between your organizations to open new doors. This means the CIO bought the CRM product and is a happy client. That will be a tremendous referral opportunity to get a meeting with the CMO about your marketing cloud offering.

Core prospects by definition already have an established relationship with your company. Taking the time to scrub your territory and prioritize accounts will pay dividends on the back end.

Tier 1 and Tier 2 Accounts. Prospects in this category of accounts do not have a relationship with your organization. However, based on certain characteristics, they're a 1 or a 2. It's hard to put a definition on the right characteristics because they're different depending on what you're selling.

Say you get a meeting with a core prospect. Just drag the contact into the Active Sales Cycle column. The idea behind this approach is that it's an easy way to stay organized, manage your business, and ensure you have some sort of interaction with each prospect in your territory every single week.

My recommendation is to send a personalized mail merge to each segment once every two weeks. Change your message for each segment. For example, if your core segment has a relationship with your organization, you should mention this in your messaging. If an account is in the lead-nurturing segment, it means they have already been through a sales cycle. Thus, you want to stop asking for a meeting and start nurturing this account with value. Eventually, they'll be open to speaking with you again. Your job is to stay top of mind, stay relevant, and add value when possible. Most importantly, ensure that no potential opportunities fall through the cracks. This system will ensure no opportunities are left behind.

How to Format Columns and Insert Personalized Attributes

The Basics of Personalized Mail Merges

What's the why behind personalized mail merges? You need a core function of automation to ensure a constant flow of discovery meetings. Remember, getting a qualified discovery meeting is the hardest part of any sales cycle. Increasing the number of qualified discovery meetings will enable you to make more money. Personalized mail merges allow you to reach everyone in your territory with a click of a button.

In technology sales, you're going to get extremely busy. I'm a firm believer that you could be busy for six straight months without doing any revenue-generating activity. Those of you who are tenured know what I am talking about; you have internal meetings, forecasting, proposals, training, and meetings about the meetings.

This book is about how to make incredible money in technology $ales, not how to stay busy. It's great that you have a ton of prospect meetings this week. However, you cannot let your outbound activity slip just because you have prospect meetings. If you let your outbound activity slip, you're going to pay the price in the following weeks with white calendar space. Calendar white space is not good for your checking account.

It's important you don't take this out of context and get lazy. This means you do not solely rely on mail merges to drive your discovery meetings. You should have a best-of-breed approach based on the segmentation of your sales territory. For example, I would never mail merge a top-ten account. These accounts require an even deeper level of personalization.

Implementing a core function of automation will be vital to achieving greatness. You've heard me say it, but I'll say it again: In technology sales, TIME is YOUR BIGGEST LIABILITY. You have 365 days a year to overachieve your quota. You must follow a system that allows you to spend your time wisely. Personalized mail merges are the core function of the automation process.

As with everything, the devil is in the details. Implementing bad mail merges that in essence look like a mail merge will hurt you more than it will help you. Everyone reading this book knows what a bad mail merge looks like. You probably get several of them every single day.

Messaging Strategy for Personalized Mail Merges

Many reps fail to take a step back and analyze why they got the meeting in the first place. Before I explain the key characteristics of what great looks like from a messaging strategy, we first need to discuss the three goals we want to achieve. Goal one is to get the email opened. Goal two is to get the email read. Goal three is to get a yes to a discovery meeting. Take a step back and start thinking about this one-two-three goal approach. If you think this way, you will change your messaging strategy for the better. Let me explain:

Goal one. Get the email opened. What makes you open an email on your desktop or your mobile device? There are several factors, but the common denominator is personalization. The spot in which the personalized attributes are placed is critical to achieving goal number one. A few pages ago, I showed you how to create personalized attributes. If you missed it, go back and watch this video first. When you send a mail merge, you want to place a personalized attribute in the first sentence every single time. Why? Because the first goal is to get the email opened. When you send an email, your prospect will most likely get the notification below in the bottom right-hand corner of his or her desktop.

Right off the bat, you can see the two personalized attributes—the company name (Baycare) and the prospect's home state (GA). These are the micro details that will improve your responses.

Prospect's View of Email from Desktop

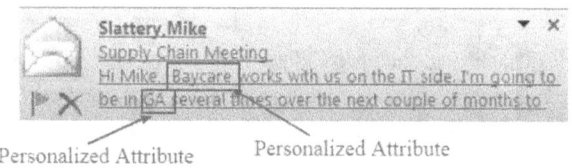

Slattery, Mike
Supply Chain Meeting
Hi Mike, Baycare works with us on the IT side. I'm going to be in GA several times over the next couple of months to

Personalized Attribute   Personalized Attribute

Prospect's view of email from a mobile device

● **Slattery, Mike** Personalized Attribute 11:09 AM »
Supply Chain Meeting
Hi Mike, Baycare works with us on the IT side.
I'm going to be in GA several times over the ne...

✎ **Slattery, Mike** Personalized Attribute Yesterday ›

The same is true on the prospect's mobile device. Two personalized attributes are visible without the prospect ever opening the email.

Messaging Strategy—Rules to Live By

1. At least one personalized attribute in the first sentence (discussed above).
2. No more than one hundred words. Why? The first reason is that when you go over a hundred words, your prospect will assume you did not individually reach out. Second, the majority of emails are opened on a mobile device. Anything over a hundred words will give you bad formatting and decrease your response chances. Until you get a feel for how long a hundred words is, start writing your prospecting emails in Microsoft Word. There is a word count on the bottom left-hand corner of the page.
3. Three to five personalized attributes in your message. It's impossible to advise the exact message you should send, as every value proposition is different. The message in the first email will be different from the tenth. In the next chapter, we'll discuss this in greater detail and introduce you to journey mapping. The main takeaway here is that five personalized attributes will increase our response rates.

Putting It All Together: Beating the Human Spam Filter

Hi Insert First Name,   Before Merge

"Company Name" works with us on the IT side. I'm going to be in "insert State" several times over the next couple of months to meet with your supply chain peers. We're working with supply chain teams from 58+ organizations. I would welcome the opportunity to meet you in person, discuss "Company Name" supply chain initiatives, and show you how we can help lower your "Insert Supply Expense" supply expense via process improvement.

Can I work with your executive assistant to schedule 45 minutes next time I'm in "insert State"?

All the Best,

Mike Slattery

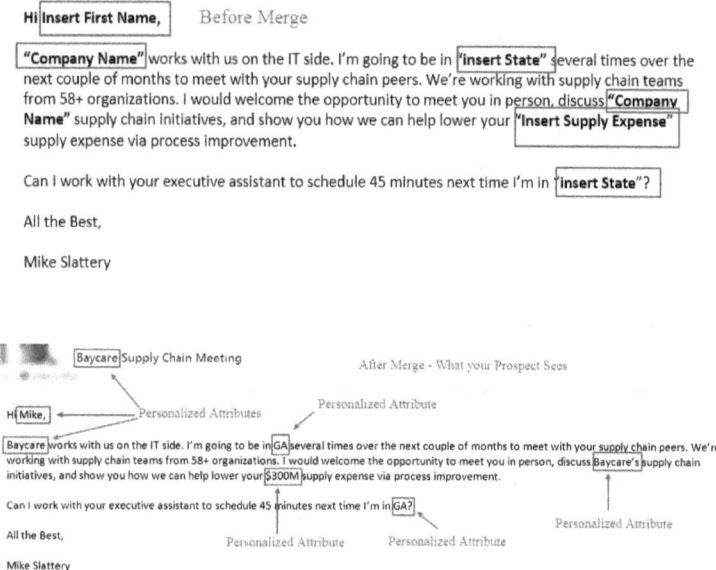

Email notification:

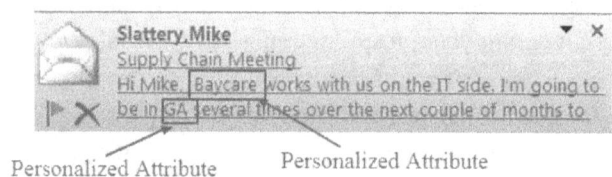

How it reads on a mobile device before opened:

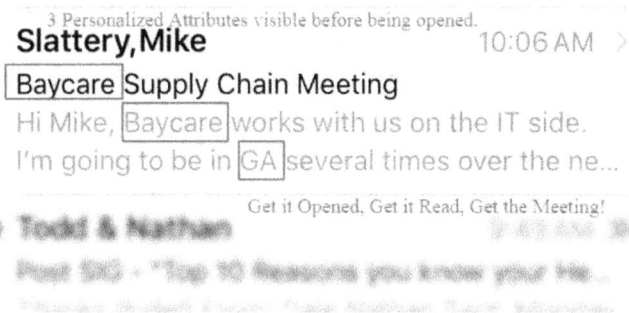

How it reads on a mobile device when opened:

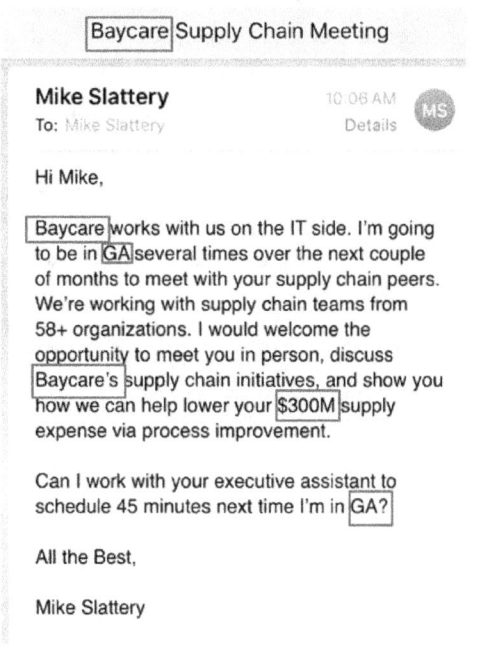

Humans have built-in spam filters. In less than a fraction of a second, your prospect is subconsciously filtering your messaging and determining whether he or she should read it line by line.

Therefore, the first step is to avoid having your prospect filter you out. The best way to do this is to insert personalized attributes such as "Company Name OR Baycare," as opposed to YOUR company.

With tools such as Yesware, you can analyze if your emails are opened on a desktop or a mobile device. I was shocked when I found that over 60 percent of my emails were being opened via mobile devices.

Another Personalized Mail Merge Example

It looks personalized because I've added personalized attributes such as the company name. It's also short enough that it looks as if it were written individually. Lastly, ensure you're giving more than you're asking when communicating with your prospects. Remember this: the higher the executive prospect, the less time he or she has to speak with you. Therefore, if you're going after the enterprise market, you must give, give, give and stop asking all the time. If you give enough value, eventually you'll get the meeting.

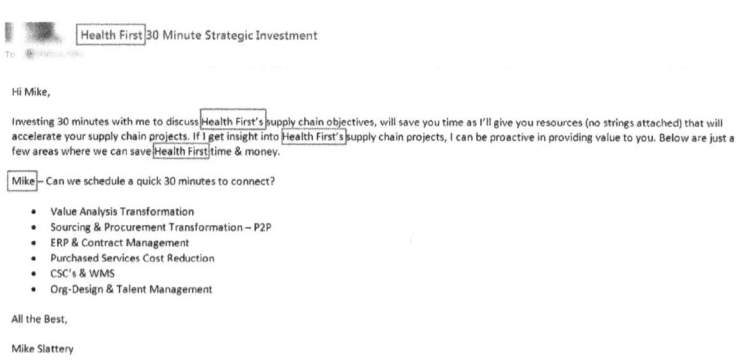

Try This Exercise

Create your best prospecting email from your desktop and send it to yourself. Then open the email on your mobile device. You see the difference in formatting?

The rule of thumb for creating great prospecting emails is to have a mobile-first approach. Use bullet points, be clear and concise, and use personalized attributes. Remember, your first goal isn't for the prospect to read your email. Your first goal is to get your prospect not to filter you out and to open your email. Lastly, don't send any links in your prospecting emails for the first five touches. If you send links too early in the process, you might find yourself in a spam filter.

We'll talk more about tools such as Yesware later in this book. One of Yesware's features is that it allows you to host documents in the cloud. You can then send your prospect links to these files. There are various benefits to this and Yesware that we'll discuss in the next chapter. It's very important that you be strategic when sending links to your prospects. Getting stuck in a spam filter can destroy your long-term email deliverability success.

Executing Personalized Mail Merges to Generate Discovery Meetings
Video – Execute Personalized Mail Merges (Refer to e-book for video link)

I'm going to show you how to send personalized mail merges at scale. As you can see below, there is no way anyone would believe this was a mail merge. This will increase your pipeline consistency and response rates when it's done right.

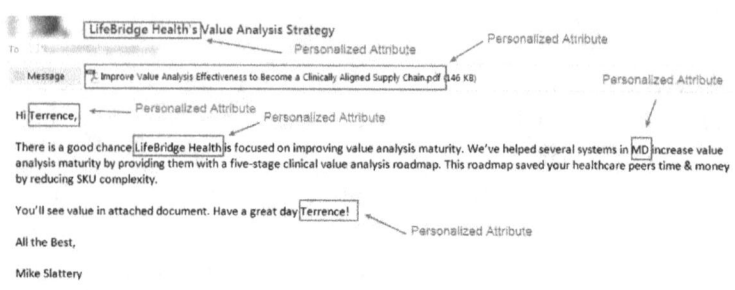

Add-On for subject-line personalization and attaching files to mail merges

Mapilab.com makes a widget called Mail Merge Toolkit. It costs twenty-four dollars per year. This toolkit allows you to personalize the subject line and add attachments. Personalizing the subject line at scale will improve your response ratios.

Download it and select Microsoft Outlook Add-Ins and Mail Merge Toolkit from the drop-down menu.

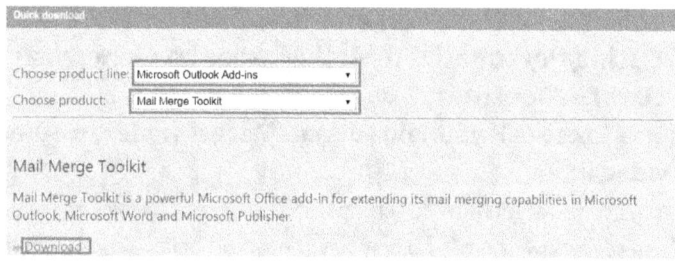

Best practice: Always test the mail merge out on yourself. The last thing you want to do is mass merge with typos, bad formatting, and so on.

Step 1

Open Microsoft Office and Microsoft Outlook.

Step 2

In Microsoft Word, go to Mailings.

Step 3

Go to Select Recipients. Then, on the drop-down menu, select Choose from Outlook Contacts. Microsoft Word will pull from your Outlook contacts.

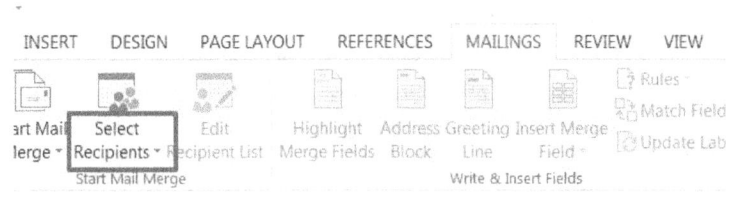

Step 4

Select the segment of contacts you want to email. Again, I would recommend creating a segment in Outlook called "mail merge test" and sending it to yourself first. For this exercise, I'm going to select my core prospects segment.

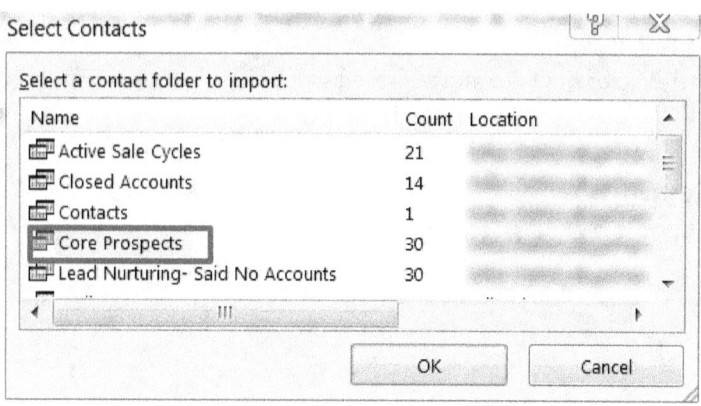

Earlier in the book, I discussed the importance of segmenting your prospects in Outlook. The recommended segment categories were Active Sales Cycles, Pending Discoveries, Lead-Nurturing Accounts, Core Prospects, Tier 1, and Tier 2. The best practice here is to create unique messaging for each of these segments. For example, we stated that core prospects already have a relationship with your organization or spend money with you. We also stated that it's always easier to sell to an existing customer than to a pure net new logo. Thus, your messaging to core prospects should reference that your companies already do business together.

Step 5

Confirm the contacts. It will show their names, companies, and so on.

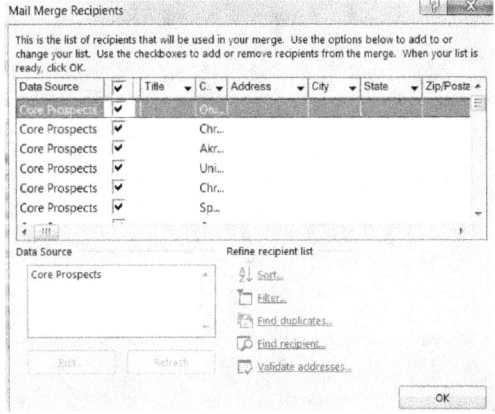

Step 6

Click Start Mail Merge. Don't worry; it won't send it out yet. Then select email messages.

Step 7

Click Greeting Line and then select None—see below.

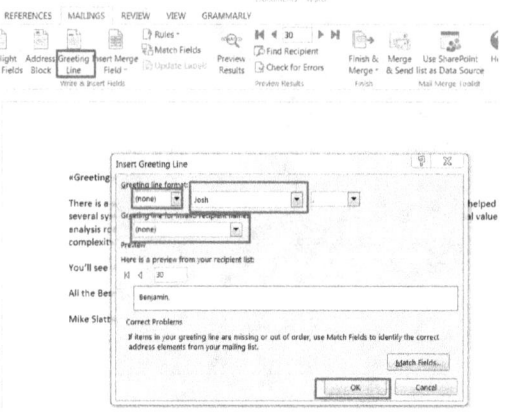

Step 8

Highlight in your messaging the words you want to change. I've high-lighted "your company." Click the drop-down menu on the tab Insert Merge Field. You'll see several options. I've chosen to insert the company name, which will add a level of personalization to our mail merge.

Below is what you'll see after the Insert Merge Field selection is complete.

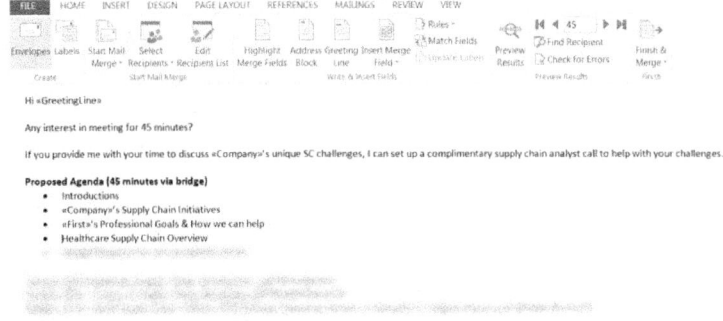

Step 9

Click Preview Results. This is what your prospects will see. You can click each of the blue arrows to the right to preview each contact's personalized message.

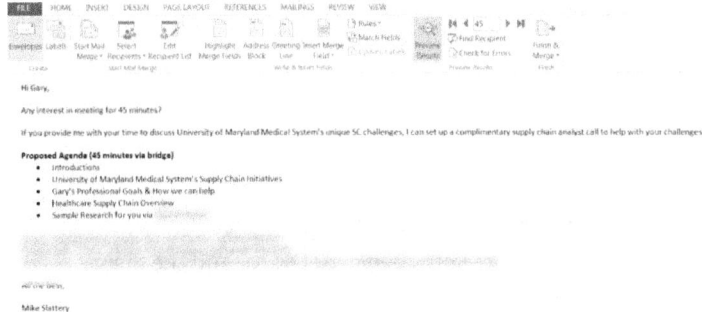

Step 10

Now we're going to insert a custom subject line and attach a file.

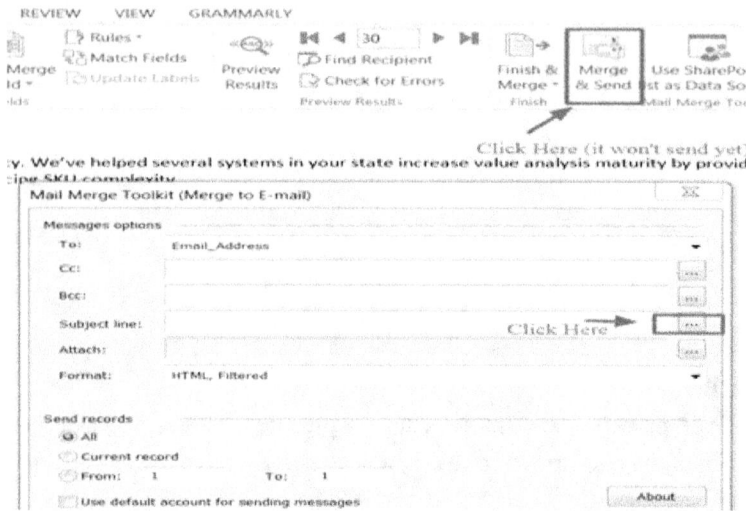

Click Finish & Merge, and then click Send Messages (don't worry; it won't send just yet).

Step 11

This is the final step (hitting the OK button sends the merge).

Create your subject line. Then click OK to send the merge.

Video—Mail Merges Using Gmail & Yesware (Refer to e-book for video link)

CHAPTER 3

Prospect Journey Mapping—The Most Efficient Way to Generate New Business

Prospect Journey Mapping

What is a prospecting journey? By definition, a prospecting journey is the complete sum of experiences a prospect experiences from the first reach out to when he or she signs an agreement. If you want to make $200,000, $300,000, or even $500,000 plus year over year, you must be strategic. Tactical execution is part of the job, but you must take the time to think about your long-term messaging strategy.

The best way to think about prospect journey mapping is this: From the first moment I reach out to the moment the prospect signs a contract, what is it that my prospect needs to know about my value proposition?

I'll say it again: What is it that my prospect needs to know about my value proposition? The reality is that it might take you ten, thirty, forty, or more touches to get a meeting. If you don't think about your messaging strategically, you'll end up not staying organized, which will lead to you sending redundant messages, which will show your prospect you're lazy, which will ultimately lead to fewer meetings and less money for you.

I closed a $120,000-plus net new logo last week. It took forty-nine emails before I got the meeting with the chief supply chain officer. I know what you're thinking—forty-nine emails. How could you possibly spend that much time on a single prospect? Forty-nine emails seems aggressive. Was your prospect annoyed with you?

To answer the questions above, it wasn't that much time at all. I started this prospect journey with a series of automated personalized mail merges and ensured I was providing some value along the way. I delivered value by inserting relevant market reports via a Yesware link. I rarely have a prospect ask to unsubscribe from my emails because I provide value along the way and personalize the messaging.

Here's the best part about this process. By the time I met with my prospect in person, he was very well educated on the value of my product offering. During the meeting, I started to wonder who was selling whom. In fact, the sales cycle was a breeze once I had the initial meeting. I didn't get lucky or receive a blue bird from the commission gods. The deal was attributed to the forty-nine well-thought-out, strategically placed messages about the value we could provide to him. Because of this, we had a very quick sales cycle that resulted in a happy client and a happy sales professional.

Prospect Journey Mapping Execution—Strategic Personalized Messaging That Will Get You the Meeting

I want you to send a reoccurring invite to yourself for two to four hours on the first of every month. During these two to four hours, I want you to map out your prospect's journey for the next six to eight weeks.

Again—what is it that your prospect needs to know about your value proposition? In other words, what are six to eight pain points that your offering solves?

Once you've uncovered these six to eight areas, I want you to write six prospecting emails with the focus on the six problems that you solve. At the time of this writing, the top six areas that are listed below in the middle of the diagram are the top pain points we solve for the health-care supply chain. The focus of my next seven touches will be around the areas listed in the diagram below. This ensures I don't send redundant messaging and that I've covered all areas of value in which we can deliver.

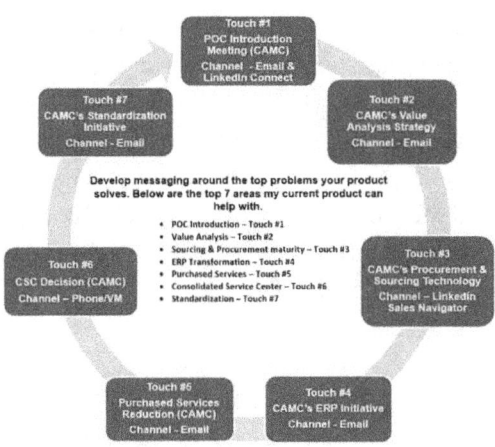

* **Send each touch separately every one to two weeks. Send on Tuesdays, Wednesdays, or Thursdays.**

Email remains the most effective channel for prospecting. However, it's important to have a multichannel approach to ensure greater results. Here, I've used a fictitious prospect (CAMC). I've mapped out the next seven interactions. You'll notice there is a sequence to the messaging. You want to identify the top business problems that your technology offering solves and reverse engineer the messaging to highlight those business problems. It's important that you sell on business problems you solve, not the functionality that you offer. All of the email outreach in this example is via mail merge. Now that you've downloaded the mail merge toolkit (last chapter), you can insert the company's name into the subject line, which is true personalization at scale.

Our sequence order is the point-of-contact introduction and a LinkedIn connection. Always send a LinkedIn invite after the first outreach; it helps puts a face to the name and lets your prospect know you're an actual human being. Touch number two is an email, and then we're going to use a different channel for touch number three—LinkedIn Sales Navigator. Touches four and five are email. Then, touch number six is phone or voice mail. Touch number seven is back to email.

Don't get too caught up in the order of the channels; you want to ensure you have a multichannel approach. The reason behind the multichannel approach is that it's more effective for getting meetings. Second, one of your channels might be broken, and you'll never know it. For example, all your voice mails might be screened out by a gatekeeper, or your email is getting stuck in spam. The multichannel strategy helps you diversify your prospecting efforts.

Seven-Touch Example of Journey Mapping at Scale

Note: Anything in **bold** represents a personalized attribute that can be inserted with a click of a button via mail merge. I'm leaving it in **bold**

simply for Illustration purposes. You'll also notice we're not always asking for an action. In fact, many times we're providing value by giving a market report or use case.

The messaging below discusses the business problems we solve and the results of solving those problems. Sell on business problems, sell on personal value, but do not sell on functionality.

In the last chapter, we discussed the messaging strategy and rules to live by. Those rules were

- at least one personalized attribute in the first sentence,
- no more than a hundred words, and
- three to five personalized attributes in your message.

Subject: POC Introduction Meeting (**CAMC**)
Word Count: 81
Ask or Give: Ask
Touch #1
Channel: Email

Hi **John,**
CAMC spent **$500 million** on supplies last year alone. Fifty-five health-care systems collaborate with us to improve operational performance around:

- Value Analysis
- Sourcing and Procurement Maturity
- ERP Transformation
- Purchased Services
- Consolidated Service Center
- Standardization

If you provide me with forty-five minutes to discuss **CAMC's** supply chain initiatives, I'll ensure you leave smarter by providing you our latest research on the topics listed above.

John, can I work with your executive assistant to schedule a time?

All the best,
Mike Slattery
XXX—Director of Business Development
555-555-5555

Subject: **CAMC's** Value Analysis Strategy
Word Count: 72
Ask or Give: Give
Touch # 2
Channel: Email

Hi **John,**
There is a good chance **CAMC** is focused on improving value analysis maturity. We've helped several systems in **GA** increase value analysis maturity by providing them with a five-state clinical value analysis road map. This road map has saved your health-care peers time and money by reducing SKU complexity.

You'll see value in the link below. Have a great day, **John!**
Insert—Usecase document via Yesware here.

All the best,
Mike Slattery
XXX—Director of Business Development
555-555-5555

Subject: **CAMC's** Procurement and Sourcing Technology
Word Count: 88
Touch #3
Ask or Give: Give

Hi **John**,
There are only so many ways **CAMC** can reduce its **$500 million** supply expense without sacrificing the quality of care. Procurement and sourcing technologies are critical components to achieving cost reduction at scale. We've helped several systems in **GA** quickly navigate the procurement technology landscape and objectively determine which vendor is best for their needs.

Attached is a great starting point for navigating the procurement and sourcing landscape.

Insert—Use case document via Yesware here.

All the best,
Mike Slattery
XXX—Director of Business Development
555-555-5555

Subject: **CAMC's** ERP Initiative
Word Count: 116
Touch #4
Ask or Give: Both

Hi **John,**
If **CAMC** is pursuing an ERP initiative over the next twenty-four months, we should connect. ERP is a huge financial investment and can tie up many of your resources. We can help **CAMC**

objectively source the right vendor and save you money via contract review. On average, we save our clients 15 percent on the majority of contracts we review. Attached is a great starting point for reducing ERP cost.

Insert—Use case document via Yesware here.

If you give me forty-five minutes to discuss your upcoming technology investments, I can provide value by sharing resources similar to the attachment.

Is there a good time to speak for forty-five minutes?

All the best,
Mike Slattery
XXX—Director of Business Development
555-555-5555

Subject: Purchased Service Reduction **(CAMC)**
Word Count: 92
Touch #5
Ask or Give: Both

Hi **John,**
Purchased services accounted for 40 percent of total supply chain cost. I estimate your supply chain expense was around **$500 million** last year. We've helped several **VPs of supply chain** reduce their PS number by creating a PS-reduction road map.

The road map below will help you get buy-in to expand your supply chain's span of control and prioritize PS-reduction targets. This is the tip of the iceberg regarding the value we can deliver to **CAMC.**

If you have other supply chain initiatives, I welcome the opportunity learn about them and discuss how we can help.

Insert—Use case document via Yesware here.

All the best,
Mike Slattery
XXX—Director of Business Development
555-555-5555

Subject: CSC Decision **(CAMC)**
Word Count: 99
Touch #6
Ask or Give: Ask

Hi **John,**

As **CAMC** evaluates strategic investments, one item might be determining if building a CSC is worth the capital outlay. We can help you determine the advantages and disadvantages of a CSC. If you do build a CSC, we can help you objectively determine which WMS provider is best for your needs. We can also review the WMS contract and save **CAMC** money. If you're going down the CSC path, I'd welcome the opportunity to show you how we can help.

Is there a good time to connect for forty-five minutes? Have a great day, **John!**

All the best,
Mike Slattery
XXX—Director of Business Development

Subject: **CAMC's** Standardization Initiative
Word Count: 80
Touch #7
Ask or Give: Both

Hi **John,**
One way **CAMC** can reduce costs is by standardizing products and reducing SKUs. One of our deliverables is a platform for learning from your peers. We've identified health-care organizations that are innovating in certain areas. Applying this knowledge to **CAMC's** supply chain will accelerate your projects by not reinventing the wheel. Below is one small example of these innovations.

If you can educate me on what you're working on, I can be more relevant in providing value.

Insert—Use case document via Yesware here.

All the best,
Mike Slattery
XXX—Director of Business Development
555-555-5555

Don't expect a ton of meetings right off the bat unless you have a kick-ass product with all the brand equity in the world. Yes, I would love to get a meeting for every outreach. However, that's not reality. In fact, you probably won't get very many meetings at all right off the bat.

However, over time your prospects are going to start becoming very well educated with your value, even if they don't have any of the problems that your product solves today. One day they will, and when they do, you want them to think of you first.

Create a Journey for Each of Your Territory Segments

Territory Segments—Active Sales Cycles, Lead-Nurturing Accounts, Core Prospects, Tier 1, and Tier 2.

By now, you have your prospecting messages mapped out across multiple channels. If you want to take this a step further, I recommend creating a journey map for each of the segment categories I discussed earlier. Those categories were Active Sales Cycles, Pending Discoveries, Lead-Nurturing Accounts, Core Prospects, Tier 1, and Tier 2. Obviously you're not asking for a meeting from one of your active sales cycles. However, out of sight is out of mind. So if you're waiting on a decision from one of your active sales cycles, you should be providing value by offering content and collateral.

Calendarize It

Put each of the messages you created on your calendar (purple Illustration below). Putting them on the calendar has several benefits. (1) It holds you accountable for hitting your desired activity levels. (2) By inserting the messaging in the calendar invite, you'll never have to worry about sending redundant messages to prospects. I can go into my calendar and see what journey-mapping strategy I ran two years ago.

If you don't want them on your calendar, save your prewritten prospecting emails to your signatures. What you're doing is creating a system that ensures your activity level never slips. You're going to get busy—that is a guarantee in technology sales.

My objective is to teach you a system where it's very easy for you to drive consistent massive outreach. By now, you understand how to create personalized mail merges. We have your database of contacts uploaded into Outlook or Gmail. You've created personalized attributes and segmented your territory.

Think of it this way: you've completed the heavy lifting. You now have the muscle mass to show as a result of the heavy lifting. Building the muscle is the hardest part; now all you need to do is maintain it. By pre-writing your next six touches, you're ensuring a system that will make it very easy for you to drive massive outreach. Save those next outreaches on your calendar or in your signatures. Now all you have to do is hit a few buttons. Regardless of how busy you get, you're never too busy to hit a few buttons.

Get your prospects journey on the calendar (Purple)

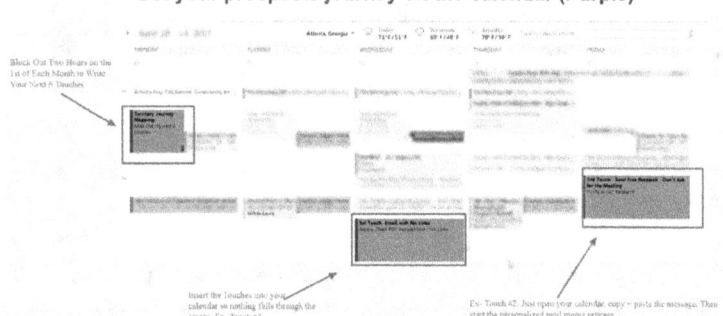

CHAPTER 4

Selling in the Digital Era Requires Digital Tools

Yesware—How to Break into Any Account

Note: Data laws change all the time. Ensure you allow your prospects to opt out, and check with your employer before using tools such as Yesware. Yesware is a cost-effective email tracking tool that will tell you who is opening your messages, links, and attachments in real time. Yesware also provides analytics on attachments your prospects are reading.

Let's say you got your top-ten must-win accounts for the year. No matter what you do, you can't seem to find a way into this account. You've called, mailed, begged the gatekeeper. You even offered a ticket to a free event. No matter what you do, you just can't seem to break into the account.

Well, my friends, let me teach you how to fish. And no, I'm not talking about phishing in the sense of hacking or anything illegal. I'm talking about knowing what your prospect is interested in without ever speaking to them.

Example: CAMC is a fictitious account, and you've identified it as top-ten must-win. You've tried your typical outreach with little results. It's now time to leverage technology to figure out what your prospect is most interested in. Start by creating the prospecting email below, and with Yesware, five cloud-hosted files have been inserted. Each inserted PDF file is a different topic area in which you can provide value. The goal here is to find out what your top-tier prospect is interested in.

Another example: If you work for Salesforce, you could insert content around all your different offerings, such as CRM, Commerce Cloud, and Marketing Cloud. Or you could insert different use cases for your offering. Click Here to get started with Yesware for Outlook.

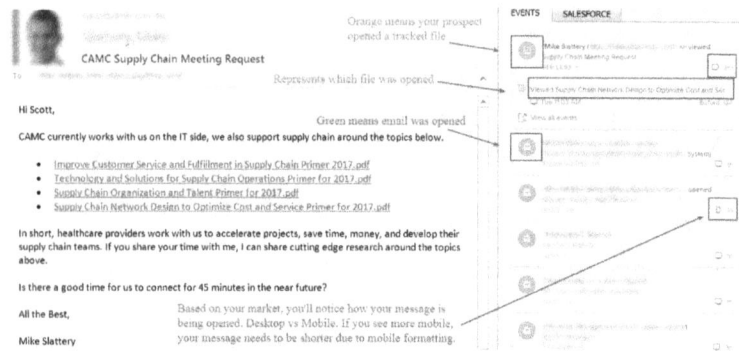

Example of Sent Email Using Yesware

Yesware integrates into your Outlook email. The green represents opened emails. You can also see whether your email was opened on a desktop or mobile device. The orange notification represents a tracked file that was opened. For this exercise, I sent the email to myself. That's why you're seeing my name on the top right.

Once you see the orange notification, click View all events.

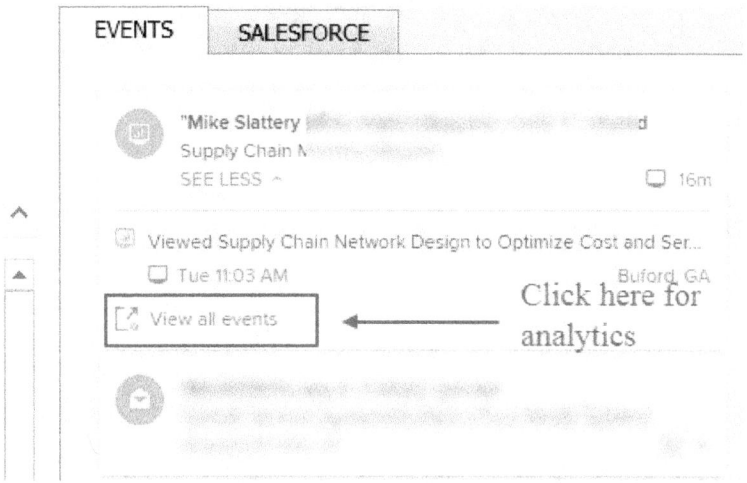

Then click on View Report.

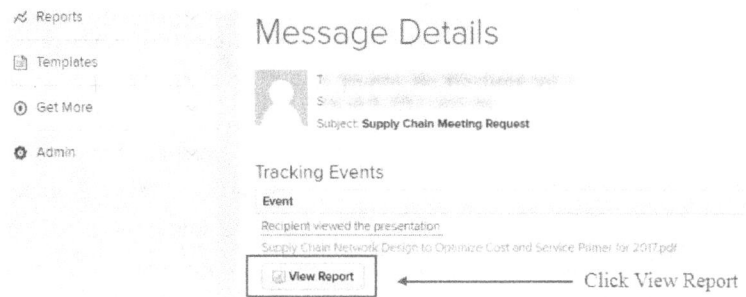

Below is the report you'll see.

Breaking Down the Value in This Report

As you may recall, this is a top-tier account that we have not been able to break into. Regardless of our online investigation efforts, we don't know what areas are of interest to our prospect. That is, until now!

Listed below are the four files we inserted into our prospecting email. By leveraging Yesware's analytics, we now know that our prospect is interested in "supply chain network design." How do we know this? Because this is the only file they opened, and they spent forty seconds on page 1, thirty seconds on page 2, and twenty-seven seconds on page 3. The other three files were left untouched or unopened.

This type of information is gold! We know our executive prospect is interested in supply chain network design. Therefore, every message from here on out is going to focus on supply chain network design. Your company should have some collateral-use cases; insert your use cases for this exercise or leverage other value-added content. This is great for sales professionals who have only ten or so accounts. The reason is that since you have only ten, you must find a way to break into the accounts that you have. If you do this right, you can get a meeting with anybody.

Hi Scott,

CAMC currently works with us on the IT side, we also support supply chain around the topics below.

- Improve Customer Service and Fulfillment in Supply Chain Primer 2017.pdf
- Technology and Solutions for Supply Chain Operations Primer for 2017.pdf
- Supply Chain Organization and Talent Primer for 2017.pdf
- Supply Chain Network Design to Optimize Cost and Service Primer for 2017.pdf

In short, healthcare providers work with us to accelerate projects, save time, money, and develop their supply chain teams. If you share your time with me, I can share cutting edge research around the topics above.

Is there a good time for us to connect for 45 minutes in the near future?

All the Best,

Mike Slattery

Video—How to Track Files in Outlook (Refer to e-book for video link)

Other Ways to Leverage Yesware—Condensing Content—One Hundred Slides into One

We'll discuss the discovery process in the next chapter. One of the common challenges in the discovery process is not having enough time to understand all of your prospect's needs. You might get a few of their initiatives, but it's a challenge to get every single one with the little time you have.

When you don't get everything you need in the discovery, there is a tendency to add more slides during the solution meeting. If you don't know this already, you can't present a fifty-slide deck (death by PowerPoint) during the solution meeting.

Alternately—my favorite situation—your prospect tells you all their challenges during a discovery meeting, and then, by the time you're ready to have the solution/proposal meeting, those areas are no longer challenges.

Yesware allows you to host sales collateral in the cloud. PowerPoint is still king, and I don't believe you should ever use more than twelve to fifteen slides in your presentations. However, sometimes your prospect will throw you a curveball, and you'll need to adjust. Yesware allows you to condense your sales content so you can provide more content with fewer slides.

Example

This is a single slide from the sales deck I created. However, this single slide contains roughly one hundred slides in one. Selling this way allows me to go wherever the conversation takes me. Also, it provides a better experience for the prospect when you're not in the room.

I don't work for Yesware, and Yesware does not pay me. I'm simply a fan of Yesware, as their technology helps me make money.

CHAPTER 5

Mastering the Discovery Meeting—This Is Where Deals Are Won and Lost

Everything we've been discussing has been focused on helping you get more qualified discovery meetings. From building your resiliency fire to prospect journey mapping, you now have a strong, consistent system in place for getting the meeting. As discussed, getting the initial meeting is the hardest part of the sale. The more discovery meetings you have, the more opportunities you'll have to make money.

Now we're going to shift gears and focus on the second critical component of the equation, which is improving your close ratio. If you become great at generating new opportunities and closing the existing opportunities, then you will make an incredible amount of money.

For all the newbies out there, the discovery meeting is, essentially, the first meeting with your prospect. Executives are extremely busy, and realistically, you're the last person on their list of priorities. In other words, you had better bring your A game to this meeting because deals are won and lost in the discovery meeting.

When you get time with executives, you need to demonstrate unwavering confidence and conviction in the value you can deliver to them. Have you ever met a salesperson who lacks confidence in the products he or she is selling? Of course you have. You probably determined within thirty seconds that this is not the type of person you want to do business with.

So what breeds confidence? In the words of Deion Sanders, "If you look good, you feel good, and when you feel good, you play good." Confidence starts with your appearance. Sounds basic, right? You wouldn't believe how many reps I've met rocking their 1990s suits. You need to invest in yourself, and that includes your appearance. If you don't have the money, finance a well-tailored suit.

Beyond the basics of looking sharp, preparation and practice are the best way to breed confidence. When you've done your homework, you instantly add credibility with your prospects.

How to Prepare for a Discovery Meeting

Let's cover the basics. The first step is connecting with your prospect on LinkedIn weeks before the meeting. Why? Because you want to allow time for your prospect to accept your invitation. There is value in being connected with your executive prospects via LinkedIn. For instance, when a prospect accepts your invitation, you can see whom he or she is connected to as well as any shared connections. Whatever technology you decide to sell, you'll soon find that it's a small world. Odds are your prospects have relationships with some of your company's current clients.

The key is knowing which current clients are advocates of your product. Most companies will have a list of go-to references. Back to the value of the LinkedIn connection: Now that you've connected with your prospect before the meeting, you start browsing through his or her LinkedIn connections and notice your prospect is connected to three of your client advocates on LinkedIn. Write those names down!

No matter how good your business case is or how good you're at sales, your prospect may take what you say with a grain of salt. This is perfectly OK. I'm in sales, and my objective is to sell you something. I know it, you know it, and your prospect knows it.

There's nothing more powerful than saying, after you present your proposal and business case, "I noticed you were connected to (insert connected client advocates here) on LinkedIn. They were skeptical at first, but they are now advocates of our product. I recommend you reach out to them and ask how we delivered value to them." Even if your prospect doesn't reach out, you've just added a tremendous amount of credibility. Also, FOMO (fear of missing out) is real. If you say so and so is doing it, others are likely to follow. It's human nature. Note: Make sure you follow your company's policy regarding name dropping or leveraging any current client's information. You'll typically need approval from the client.

Premeeting Prep

Your first stop is always LinkedIn. Why? Because your prospect wrote the material on his or her LinkedIn landing page. Build rapport by seeing where your prospect went to school, what groups he or she belongs to, and his or her potential interests, job responsibilities, previous employers, and length of time at their current company.

As we discussed earlier, you already know whether this is a pure net new logo because of how you tiered your territory. If there is an existing relationship, check your CRM and ensure you understand how long they've been a client. Also, you want to know the value delivered to other departments and try to connect with your colleagues to better understand any previous sales cycles with the company.

Public Companies vs. Private Companies Premeeting Plan

By now you've done the premeeting basics. If your prospect is a publicly traded company, this section will be a lot easier. All public companies will publish an annual report. If I were stranded on an island, I'd rather talk to a volleyball named Wilson than read through these reports. However, these reports are valuable, and there are a few things you want to look for using the Control+F function (Control+F will search for keywords).

The first is their fiscal year end. When you're selling to enterprise or Fortune 1000 companies, it can be very difficult for the organization to move budget around. It's not impossible, but you'll need to uncover some serious pain your product solves for this to happen. Alternatively, you might be able to identify some discretionary budget that your prospect has.

However, there is only so much discretionary budget, and this book is about making incredible money in technology sales. Thus, we're selling big-ticket items. Moreover, if we're selling big-ticket items, you will need to know when your prospect starts and ends their budgeting process. Knowing this information will also help you be proactive in offering customized solutions if your prospect does not have the budget now.

For example, offering net ninety billing terms when they're three months from their new fiscal will allow them to get started now and fund the purchase ninety days from now. Remember, time kills all deals. I'll always take one dollar today than the promise of two dollars tomorrow. Offering proactive solutions to get the deal done starts with knowing basic details such as their fiscal year end.

I've sold to emerging tech companies whose budget process consisted of three people meeting in a tiny huddle room and to the CIO of a Fortune 500 company whose budgeting process started six months before the calendar year end. If you're selling to the enterprise, it will always be easier to close the deal if you get in the budget on the front end as opposed to asking your prospect to fight internally to pull the budget from somewhere else.

Best practice tip: If you're selling to publicly traded companies, one of your tiering factors should be their fiscal year end. If your company has a December fiscal year end, start targeting that company six months out (June) to improve the likelihood of getting in the budget. I love when I hear "Thanks for reaching out; your timing is good." I hate when I hear "We just finalized our budgets. Reach out again next year." Not all companies are on the December fiscal year end. For instance, health-care systems' year end will typically be June, September, or December.

Back to the annual report. The strategy is going to start at the top, with the CEO. See if you can find some information about their upcoming business objectives. I'm willing to bet the farm that any CEO's top priority is growth. There are only so many ways a publicly traded company can grow. For example, they can increase revenue by acquiring new customers, have better retention of existing customers, expand into new vertical markets, expand into new geographies, and acquire revenue through company acquisition. This is the type of information you're looking for in the annual report.

Why Should You Know This Information?

At the time of this writing, I've closed 102 net new logos and conducted over a thousand discovery meetings. The higher up the executive is, the less time you have to make an impact at advancing your sale. I'm not saying to skip the rapport building; this is important. What I'm saying is that you need to drive the conversation and not waste the little time that you have.

I cringe when I hear reps say, "Tell me about your role." Why? Because (a) you should already know everything about that person's role. You should know the detailed responsibilities of his or her job by looking at similar roles on Indeed.com or other recruiting websites. And (b) you just opened up the floodgates for your prospect to waste half the meeting on information you could have found on your own.

A better approach is to read the annual report before this meeting. You say, "Your CEO stated that improving customer experience is a top priority as it relates to your growth strategy." (Translation: What the CEO is saying is that we have a leaky bucket, and our customer experience is bad.)

Your prospect says, "Yes, improving customer experience is a top priority."

You say, "Tell me how you and your team are currently leveraging technology to improve customer experience."

In this example, your product offering improves customer experience. What did we accomplish in the first five minutes of our meeting? (a) We established credibility by showing we've done our homework. (b) Your prospect might need approval from his boss, the CEO, so let's kick off the conversation with a topic that will solve problems for your prospect and his or her boss, the CEO. (c) Most importantly, we're not wasting what little time we have, and we're discussing problems that matter.

The main point here is that doing your research will breed confidence, establish creditability, and ensure you don't waste what little time you have.

Private Companies Premeeting Plan

Private companies are tougher to prep for because they don't have to disclose a lot of the information that the publicly traded companies do. What's nice about private companies is that the sales cycles can be much quicker (but not always). Private companies seem to be more agile in general, and when they want something, they can get it done more quickly than big enterprises.

The prepping process is similar. Start with LinkedIn and try to uncover why they've chosen to stay private. I will say private companies can be a challenging sale at times for big-ticket technology items. My theory is that they don't have to grow at all year over year to be successful. If you're a C-level decision maker at a private company and your net profit was $10 million last year, you're probably perfectly OK with having a $10 million profit the next year.

Private companies don't have to grow 10 percent year over year to keep the shareholders happy, mostly because they don't have shareholders. People need a reason to change, and the reason needs to be compelling. A best practice: ask for more time during the discovery meeting with your private company prospects because you'll need to ask more basic-level questions since the information was not available online.

Discovery Meeting—Game Time

You know your product, you know your prospect, you're prepared, and you're looking sharp and ready to rock. The first person you will interact with is not your prospect, but, typically, an executive assistant. Notice I don't call them admins. Why? Would you like to be called someone's admin? Probably not. The executive assistants I've met are some of the hardest-working people on planet Earth, and they typically don't get the credit they deserve.

Furthermore, most sales reps treat them like admins and have no idea the level of influence these people have on your sales cycles. My point is to be nice, be charming, and treat executive assistants the way you would Fortune 100 CEOs. A best practice: drop them a small gift on the way in—a phone charger, a USB memory stick, cookies, or whatever it is—just do something that shows you care. This will differentiate you from 90 percent of the other five hundred reps trying to get time on your executive prospect's calendar.

Quick story: Last September, I got a verbal for a $220,000 deal. For you newer folks out there, verbals don't pay the bills. Then I got nothing but silence from my prospect. I called, emailed, direct mailed, and texted over and over. But still, nothing but awful dead silence. The kind of silence that will drive a man insane, the kind that wakes you up at night. My ace in the hole was that I had treated the executive assistant like a CEO because she deserved to be treated like one. It was Halloween, October 31st, and I sent her some cookies and wished her happy Halloween. I kid you not—two hours later, I had a signed contract sitting in my inbox. The moral of the story? Executive assistants can make or break you. Treat them like the CEO.

Now you're ready to meet with your executive prospect. Most companies have policies in place against accepting vendor gifts. So if you walk in with a pair of Super Bowl tickets for your prospect, they probably won't be able to accept them. However, small gifts are typically OK. I like to walk in with a Tervis tumbler that has my company's logo embroidered on it. Inside, I like to include a flash drive with any content we review that day, additional sales collateral, a business card, and a company embroidered pen. Why? Everyone drinks water throughout the day. A Tervis tumbler has a good chance of ending up on my prospect's desk. I want them to see my company's logo every single day. Remember what I said earlier: out of sight is out of mind.

How to Kick Off the Meeting: Strong Introduction

Most discovery meetings are anywhere from thirty minutes to ninety minutes. I typically ask for forty-five minutes. Thirty minutes is too short, and it can be a challenge getting more than sixty minutes with an executive for a first meeting. We're going to pretend we got forty-five minutes. A best practice: Wear a watch so you can manage the time. Your phone should never be out.

We're assuming you've already built rapport. You researched LinkedIn to find common ground with your executive. Now you're ready to get down to business. You want to have a well-rehearsed, strong introduction to set the tone and add credibility.

Strong Introduction Example (What Good Looks Like)

Hi, Mary.
I sincerely appreciate your time. The reason I've been reaching out is that you're a perfect fit for leveraging our customer-experience platform, and I know we can provide a tremendous amount of value. The reason I believe you're a perfect fit is because we specialize in the retail vertical, and your peers such as (insert those common LinkedIn client connections here) have seen improved customer retention rates and a hard ROI as a result of leveraging our platform.

Introduction Example (What Bad Looks Like)

This is what a bad introduction looks like.

Hi, Mary.
Thank you for your time. I wanted to discuss your challenges. Once I understand your challenges, we can determine if there is alignment between your challenges and our offerings.

STOP IT! This drives me nuts as a sales professional. You just told your prospect this might be a complete waste of her time.

Why is the first example strong? Mostly because we're confident that we can absolutely provide a tremendous amount of value. We're not here to waste your time. Since we specialize in the retail vertical, we understand your world, and we're here to help. Furthermore, I promise that when you name drop their peers who are already working with you, you'll have their attention for the rest of the meeting. Again, set the tone of the meeting and drive the conversation. If you're nervous, just fake it until you make it.

Introduction to Agenda Transition

I've done as much research as I can on your company to maximize our time together. Our technology offerings can help in a hundred different ways, but I don't want to boil the ocean. What I want to do is to confirm your CEO's growth strategy and discuss how you're contributing to this strategy. In addition, I would like to ask you a series of questions so I can better help you. Once I understand your unique situation, I can showcase how we're helping companies grow through improved customer retention and experience. How does that sound, and is there anything you would like to add?

Introduction to Agenda Transition Breakdown

Most reps will just start asking questions. If we only ask more questions, certainly that will increase sales. This might sound familiar to you. If you think about it, the discovery process is kind of strange. You meet someone for the first time and start asking very detailed questions about his or her job, objectives, and so on.

What you're trying to do is break down that wall and get your executive to open up. I have always found that telling your prospect why you're about to ask so many questions helps break down that wall faster. If you just go in and start firing away, you'll probably get more yes/no answers to your questions.

Agenda Transition—How to Get What You Need to Move the Ball Forward

Again, we're selling big-ticket items ($50,000 to $10 million plus). The higher the price, the more stakeholders you'll have to win over. Even if the CEO is not in the meeting, let's get information that will help us sell to the CEO/CFO and our executive prospect.

I don't like writing down a ton of questions because I can't listen if I'm thinking about the next question. Keep it simple. Try to ask questions around the three buckets below.

- **Corporate objectives**
- **Your executive prospect's objectives**
- **Personal value objectives (my favorite)**

Your talk track might look something like this:

You ask, "I know you're trying to grow 10 percent year over year. What is the primary strategy for hitting that goal?"

Your prospect says, "We've been great at acquiring new customers, but we have a retention problem. It doesn't do us any good to win customers only to lose them six months later."

You ask, "Do you know why you're losing customers?"

Your prospect says, "None of our systems communicate, our data is in silos, and we're running on outdated systems. For instance, if we have a loyal longtime customer who buys something online and then goes into one of our brick-and-mortar stores, our systems have no way of letting our employees know that this a high-priority or loyal customer."

You then want to confirm: "If you were to fix this problem, would it lead to better customer retention?"

Your prospect says, "Yes, it would."

You say, "Do you have an estimate of how many percentage points your customer retention would improve by fixing this?"

Your prospect says, "It's a tough question, but to be conservative, I'd say around 5 percent."

You say, "Can you put a figure to that 5 percent?"

Your prospect says, "Roughly $20 million in increased revenue."

Breakdown

What's good about this? From our premeeting plan, we had an idea that improving customer experience might be a priority based on the annual report. Another indication that it was a priority is that your prospect accepted the meeting, and he or she knows you sell customer-experience solutions.

We uncovered that the overall growth objective is 10 percent (what the CEO cares about). As we discussed earlier, there are only so many ways a company can grow. We uncovered that the primary growth strategy would be on retaining existing customers (still what the CEO cares about). We confirmed the current state of the problem—why our prospect has a customer retention problem. As I mentioned, people need a reason to change. It's hard for people to change when there isn't a clear financial benchmark next to the problem at hand. Therefore, we asked how fixing this would improve customer experience in a percentage format. Finally, we asked, can you put a dollar amount behind that 5 percent? And our prospect replied with $20 million.

By now we have a good understanding of the corporate objective and our executive prospect's top objective. We've positioned ourselves to solve our prospect's problem and his or her boss's problem (the CEO) without even meeting with the CEO. We even got a financial benchmark of a $20 million increase in revenue by solving this problem. This financial benchmark number will be extremely valuable when we discuss justifying the sale during the solution/proposal meeting. So it's a done deal, right? Not yet.

Personal Value—How to Create Your Internal Champion

People are not interested in you. They are not interested in me.
They are interested in themselves, morning, noon and after dinner.
—Dale Carnegie

It's very rare that you'll sell a large-ticket technology solution that has only a single decision maker. Sometimes it could be a single decision maker, but you're probably not going to get access to that person, such as the CFO or CEO. So if you can't get access to the ultimate decision maker, how are you expected to sell? You'll have to create an internal champion among the people you do have access to. So how do you create an internal champion? Does helping the massive, publicly traded company grow 20 percent make an internal champion? Probably not, unless your prospect has stock options.

You see, most reps ask so many questions about the business. They assume that their prospect cares about the business morning, noon, and after dinner. The reality in most cases is that they care most about their jobs and their family, not about the company they work for. Of course, they'll never admit it, but I call it like I see it.

I've lost deals where I thought I had the greatest business case in the world. The type of business case where you're so confident, you book that all-inclusive Jamaican vacation before the paperwork is signed. I won't make that mistake again. Then you get a no, and you just can't seem to figure out why.

This happens all the time; we do everything right and then get a no. Sure, our prospect said he or she spoke to leadership, but now was just not the right time. Sometimes I wonder if the conversation ever took place with leadership, or did my prospect just say it did?

The way to fix this problem and create an internal champion is through personal value. Personal value is about how your solution will have a personal impact on your prospect. Will your solution fix a problem that will result in your prospect getting a raise? Will your solution help your prospect do his or her job better, which leads to better performance, which typically leads back to more money for your prospect?

Discussing Personal Value in the Discovery Meeting

I mentioned the strategy of letting your prospects know up front why you're asking them questions. Doing this helps break down the communication wall. Try this talk track for personal value.

You say, "Many of our clients have seen substantial raises as a result of leveraging our product. Most of my clients receive a bonus if they can prove that they positively impacted customer retention rates. So I'm curious—how do you get a raise, and what's your main metric?"

If you ask, how do you get a raise? Without the backstory, it seems like a strange question. Delivery is everything, and we did it in a way that was disarming. It feels uncomfortable when you first ask this question, but you'll find that your prospect appreciates the fact that you asked.

You now know how your prospect gets paid and the main metrics. Now you want to showcase how your technology offering is going to help your prospect get that raise. I promise that if you do this well, you'll create an internal champion who is willing to fight to implement your technology solution.

Sales processes seem to get even more complicated as the years go by. I'm a firm believer in keeping it simple when possible. If there is one thing you take away from the discovery process, it's this: Sales are about helping people solve problems. Have you ever thought about why your prospects want to solve problems? They want to solve problems because it's their job. They have a job because they want to get paid. Thus, if you can align your solution to solve a problem and demonstrate how this might help them increase their pay, you have a really good shot at closing this sales cycle.

Closing the Discovery Strong

By now you're thirty minutes into your meeting, and you have fifteen minutes left. From a discovery standpoint, you have everything you need. We know the corporate objective is to grow by 10 percent. Their strategy is to grow via improved customer retention. Our executive prospect's top objective is to improve customer experience, which will lead to improved customer retention. We know the current state that is causing this problem, which is that none of their systems communicate, their data is in silos, and they're running on outdated systems. We even got a financial benchmark of a $20 million increase in revenue by solving this problem, and our prospect has told us she can receive a bonus if she can prove how she positively impacted customer retention rates.

So What's the Next Step?

You want to recap to your prospect what you've heard. Why? It shows that you were listening to your prospect's needs, which they will appreciate, and it allows them the opportunity to confirm or correct you if you missed something.

You Have Ten Minutes Left

Let me know if this sounds familiar. You have a phenomenal discovery meeting; you get absolutely everything you need in that meeting. Before you leave, you get the solution meeting on the calendar. Great—you're scheduled to return in two weeks to showcase how you will solve all the problems your prospect has. But then, two days before the scheduled solution meeting, your prospect pushes the meeting out three weeks. Three weeks comes around, and your prospect reschedules again for another four weeks out.

This happens all the time, and it sucks! This makes completing the sale much more challenging for two reasons. One, if your prospect reschedules for seven weeks out, there is a chance that improving customer experience is no longer a priority. Two, so much time has gone by that you basically need to do the discovery again, which means your sales cycle from hell will continue to drag out.

Rescheduling happens to all of us, and there is no 100 percent way to prevent it. However, there are some things you can do to improve the velocity of your sale cycles.

Many reps will end a discovery meeting without discussing what they can do for the prospect. They want to save it all for the solution/proposal meeting. I believe there is a balance between the two. If you think about it, you've drilled your prospect with questions for thirty minutes. You want to provide enough value during the last ten minutes to keep them interested in advancing the sales cycle or moving to the next stage. Why? If you don't give them anything, you run the risk of consistent rescheduling and a stalled sales cycle.

Remember when I talked about the power of Yesware and how you can condense a hundred slides into a single page? It's time to leverage this right now or do a very quick demo of the section that highlights how you've helped other retail-vertical customers improve their customer experience. The goal is to Illustrate very quickly how you can solve all the problems you uncovered at a high level. Unfortunately, there is no 100% sure-fire solution to prevent rescheduling.

However, if you provide enough value to your prospect and confidently articulate how you can solve their problems, you'll improve the velocity of your sales cycles. Finally, don't ever leave scheduling the next step to email. Ask your prospect if you can schedule time with the executive assistant on your way out.

CHAPTER 6

Solution—Proposal Meeting—How to Improve Your Close Ratio

N ow is a good time to discuss the role of analyst firms and how they impact your sales cycles. Gartner is the largest research-and-advisory firm providing information-technology-related insight to IT and other business leaders located across the world.

Most CIOs have access to Gartner. Gartner publishes reports called Magic Quadrants. This research note is essentially a short list of technology vendors within a particular technology market. Gartner will advise a client based on what's best for the client's needs at the given time.

Chances are your prospect read this report before speaking to you. You need to understand how Gartner views your product's strengths and its cautions. Furthermore, you need to understand your competitors' strengths and cautions based on Gartner's objective advice. Any information you present to your prospect will most likely be validated by Gartner.

You also need to understand that it's highly unlikely that you're the only vendor your prospect is speaking with. They'll have at least a handful of vendors who will make their short list before they make the final deci-sion. Therefore, it's important that you understand how Gartner views your offering and your competitors' offerings so you can quickly handle objections. We'll talk about how to use this information when selecting the right technology company to work for later in the book.

Back to the Solution—Proposal Meeting

Every organization has a different name for the solution meeting. Some call it a proposal meeting, capabilities alignment meeting, services over-view meeting, product demo meeting…and the list goes on. If you want a common framework, this is where you're taking everything you learned in your discovery meeting and making a recommendation to the client as to the right set of products based on their unique needs. Every orga-nization is different, but there are several common denominators that I consider best practices.

In every solution meeting, I try to envision myself as the prospect. The best sales professionals have a way of making the most complex technology offerings simple. To keep things simple, you want to assume your prospect doesn't understand your internal acronyms or your technology.

Another best practice is to leverage your resources. Many top per-formers are not technical experts, nor do they have anything close to the technological knowledge of a CIO. The truth is, they don't have to. Often they just need to have a decent understanding of how the tech-nology works, the business impact that it will deliver, and how it's differ-entiated from the competitive landscape. When they start getting into the weeds from an integration standpoint, they often bring in their sales engineers, who have the deep technical expertise. Another way to put it is that top-performing sales professionals are like quarterbacks. They know they can't do it by themselves. Their job is to effectively leverage the resources within their offense and drive the ball down the field.

Again, every solution meeting is different. Here are a few best practices beyond the basics.

If they're a current client and you're selling an add-on product or a whole new line of offerings, make sure you know the value delivered with the original products they bought. For example, let's say you're selling human capital management software (HCM). Let's say the chief human resource officer (CHRO) is a current client of yours (say they use you for talent management). Now you're selling a different set of products to the chief procurement officer (CPO). Try to get value statements from the current client. If you know they're fans of yours, make sure you put their name in the solution deck as a reference. Nothing is better than an internal reference.

Quick story: Have you ever met that guy in the room, the guy who has no power or authority to make a decision, yet throws every objection in the book at you? These guys are everywhere, and it's their sole purpose in life to derail every meeting and try to make you look bad.

That guy happened to be attending my solution meeting one day. I was selling to a CPO, and their CIO was an existing client of ours. That guy attempted to derail the meeting several times, and then he threw out an objection that I'll never forget. It was "Mike, you say you can help us reduce costs by learning best practices from your subject-matter experts. Truthfully, I don't see the value here. Can you name one time when you've helped any company reduce costs?"

Luckily, before the meeting, I had looked in our CRM system. I noticed we had saved their CIO $350,000 in a thirty-minute phone call. So I replied, "You know, the best example I can think of was just three weeks ago, when we saved your CIO $350,000 in thirty minutes." That guy didn't say a word for the next forty-five minutes. One month later,

I had a multiyear contract in hand for about $205,000. The moral of the story is to know the history of the organization, good or bad.

Top Tips for a Killer Solution Presentation

- Be prepared. Know everything you can about your audience.
- Dress sharp.
- Open with the executive summary—what you heard in the discovery meeting.
- Share how you've helped similar clients with the same priorities.
- Use more visuals than words.
- Use no more than fifteen slides (ten ideally; an appendix is OK).
- Help them justify the expense.

Opening to the Solution Proposal—Commanding the Meeting

You want to kick the meeting off with an executive summary. This means you want to state what you're doing here and recap everything you learned in your discovery meeting. Many reps will talk a lot about their company, but I find most buyers don't care. Instead, talk about how third-party analyst firms view your offerings. If you don't have this, discuss how similar clients have leveraged your solution to drive business value. Using these examples up front helps add objective credibility and sets the tone for the meeting.

Then you're going to take everything you've uncovered in the discovery and showcase how your technology offering is going to solve these problems. After you've done this, you must differentiate. If you cost more than your competitors, you need to have a compelling reason why. Most importantly, remind them how this product is going to provide personal value. If you do this well, you'll create an internal champion.

You could write an entire book on the right type of content to provide during the solution meeting, and everyone has a different approach. From a content standpoint, go by this rule: "Don't tell me how you can help me; show me how you can help me." Again, it's more powerful to show firsthand how your product did X for Y organization.

A best practice: At the end of the solution meeting, ask, "Is there any reason why you would not move forward?" You cannot handle an objection if you don't know what the actual objection is. Asking this question will allow your prospect to get objections out on the table.

Believe it or not, I embrace getting a no from a prospect when I understand the reasons. I can't stand when I get a no and don't understand the reason. Asking the question above will clarify where some of the roadblocks might be.

Justification of the Sale—Closing Time

Every time we make a purchase, there is a subconscious justification we all go through. The exception might be something like an impulse buy at a supermarket. In general, it's human nature to justify your actions in life. Make it easy on your prospect; don't assume they're able to justify it. Provide them with creative ways to justify the business expense and tie it back to the personal value we discussed earlier.

Technology sales are complicated, but I like to keep things simple. There are only three categories of enterprise technology products on the market if you think about it.

1. **Technology that helps the business make money.**
2. **Technology that helps the business save money.**

3. **Technology that improves operational performance, which will help make or save the business money.**

When you think about justifying the sale, keep in mind you'll probably have to justify it to the CFO. It's ideal to understand what the CFO cares about even if you've never met that person. In general, your technology offering will fit into one of the three categories above. Make sure you're clear and concise and have a visual slide allocated to justify the sale.

What Is a Justification Statement?

In a short, concise manner, help your prospect justify the amount of money you're requesting. This is my closing slide, and if there is only one slide, my prospect remembers this is it.

The better you can understand how your prospect is currently spending the business's money, the easier it will be to help them justify the sale. For example, let's say your technology fits into category three, which improves operational performance via automation of manual processes. Say your prospect is considering hiring five full-time employees (FTEs). Your technology offering is more efficient than five employees, and the cost is way less than hiring five FTEs.

Example of a Justification Statement for Your $90,000 Offering

This costs about as much annually as hiring someone directly out of college ($50,000 salary and taxes, benefits, etc.). Do you see more value in hiring an entry-level employee or implementing a product that can do the work of five employees?

A best practice: When you first get into the role, try to get your hands on a sample profit-and-loss (P&L) statement from one of your clients. If you can't get it from your clients, a P&L from the same industry and a similar-size company will work. You want to study that P&L and understand what your prospect's standard budget looks like by line item. The better you understand your prospect's budget, the better you can align your product offering to one of the line items in the budget.

Another example: Let's say my product helps businesses lower their supply chain expense. I didn't even need the P&L for this example; I found their supply cost in their annual report.

Example of a Justification Statement for a $400,000 Offering

Your supply expense last year was $1.2 billion. At the end of the day, do you believe this product will reduce your supply expense by one-tenth of 1 percent?

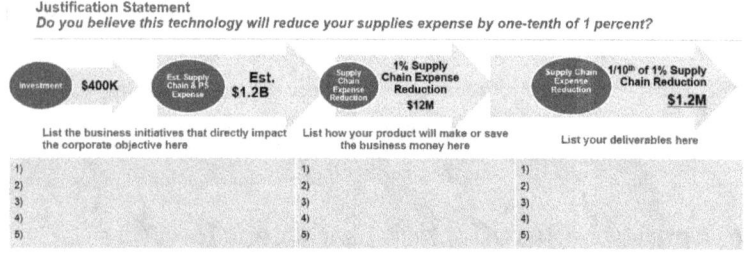

Why Is This Good?

People believe what they see, not what they hear. We're helping our prospect justify the expense. We don't have to be their savior; our goal is to close the sale. So attaching to the biggest portion of their budget will give us a greater probability of winning. What we're saying is, would you invest $400,000 if we could save you $1.2 million? Of course you would.

We didn't assume that our prospect would connect the dots; we took all the information we knew about them and put it in a visual format to help them justify the expense. Furthermore, if this goes up the ladder to the CFO, this will probably be the only slide that person looks at. Again, most technologies are designed to save money or make money. You can apply this type of framework to almost every situation. The better you understand the line items in their budget, the better you can position yourself to win.

Providing Value between Interactions—How to Stay Top of Mind

This logical next step after the solution meeting is to ask for time on the calendar regarding feedback. This might also be referred to as a reconnect, decision, or next-steps meeting. If you're not able to close them on-site, your prospect will typically state they want to have an internal discussion and that you can reconnect again in a few weeks.

Let me tell you what most reps do: most reps will send one follow up email shortly after their solution meeting and follow this with a decision-meeting calendar invite. While this is the minimum, I recommend you nurture this active prospect until they give you a decision. Moreover, if that decision is a no, continue to nurture them until that no becomes a yes.

For example, say I have a two-week window from solution meeting to decision meeting.

I would send value-added content at least weekly to stay top of mind. People are busy; don't assume your prospect is going to remember the business case you presented two weeks ago.

A best practice: If they can't decide on the spot, it's most likely because they need to have a conversation with their boss or multiple stakeholders. (The assumption is you don't have access to their boss) Before you leave, ask, "When do you expect to meet with your boss on the proposal?"

Your prospect says, "Two weeks from today."

This is fourteen days from now. You want to put a reminder on your calendar to send your prospect a Webex recording of your solution/proposal meeting twelve days from now, or two days before they meet with their boss.

Here's the problem: fourteen days, or two weeks, is a long time. I can barely remember what I did yesterday, let alone two weeks ago. This is true for your prospect; you want to make it easy for them to remember your proposal and business case. I recommend always using a Webex, even if you're presenting in person.

Why? Because you can record your proposal, solution, demo, and so on. Two days before your prospect meets with their boss, send them the Webex recorded link so they can quickly get refreshed on your meeting from two weeks ago. This will help your internal champion do a better job of selling internally, and it will also save you time by not having redundant meetings with your prospect.

CHAPTER 7

Get Ahead and Stay Ahead—How to
Improve Your Quality of Life and Stay
Ahead of Your Peers

You cannot run at 120 miles per hour without burning out at some point. I'm a huge believer in quality of life. Moreover, I've always found my quality of life improves once I've exceeded my annual quota six months into the year, or by the end of Q2. Why? Because there is no longer any pressure to perform. I've already exceeded my annual expectations to the business. Also, what you'll find is that you'll make more money and get more deals when you don't need that next deal.

I call this the anti–commission breath phenomenon. Let me explain. Have you ever seen a salesperson in December who has not hit his or her annual quota? If you have, you'll notice that 95 percent of these people have commission breath. This means they're in such a desperate situation that it can become noticeable based on their actions.

I don't know about you, but I don't like buying from desperate people. It makes me think something is wrong with the product. I like buying from confident people who know their product is so damn good that they don't even need my business. This swagger is a trait of anti-commission breath sales professionals. They don't need your money or the next deal because they hit their annual quota months ago. As a result of this, their confidence goes up, and they close more deals.

Case in point: Have you ever had a hot sales streak? This is where everything goes your way, and you feel as if the commission gods have blessed you. This isn't chance; this is because for a period, you were doing all the right things, and the results started to follow. Your confidence soared, which made you even more attractive to potential buyers.

Unfortunately, this can go both ways. You can be on the other end of the spectrum, where it feels as if you couldn't sell a boat, water, or food to man stuck on a deserted island. So then the question becomes, how do you drive consistency, avoid the cold streak, and not burn out over time?

The answer: always stay one quarter ahead of your peers. Let me give you an example. I have an annual quota, and our company's fiscal is Jan 1 through December 31. I start driving crazy outbound activity in September of the previous year. I do this because my average sales cycles takes six months. Six months from September is March, or the end of Q1. Again, I am a huge believer in living a stress-free life. And yes, contrary to popular belief, you can live a stress-free life in enterprise technology sales. You just need to get ahead of the game. Ramping up in September of the previous year allows me to have a fast start in Q1 of the upcoming year and ultimately get ahead of my peers and my quota.

I don't know about you, but vacation is so much better after all the work is done. This is why you feel more relaxed at an all-inclusive resort. It's not that the food is any better. Actually, the food is usually worse. However, you typically feel more relaxed when you stay at an all-inclusive resort. Why? Because you've put in all the work up front—or, in other words, you've already paid for everything.

There is no anxiety of high-priced meals or massive bar tabs. Even though the cost is the same, you'll feel more relaxed at an all-inclusive resort. The same thing goes for managing your sales territory. Getting ahead of the game will ultimately improve your quality of life.

Back to business—by the end of Q1 (March), I want to have hit half of my annual plan. By the end of Q2 (June), I want to have hit my annual quota. I typically take two to three weeks of vacation in April to recharge and avoid burnout. Then I bust my tail in late April, May, and June. From here, life is good and stress free.

I'll typically take my foot off the gas during July, which is ideal because most of my prospects will be on vacation as well. Then I start to ramp back up as I approach the month of August, and the cycle repeats itself.

Stress is the real killer in life; it will kill you if you let it get the best of you. Getting ahead of where you need to be will dramatically improve your quality of life, and you'll close more deals as a result of your confidence being through the roof.

Territory Planning and Creating Goal Timelines to Fuel Motivation

Most technology sales professionals sell strategic products that are very complex in nature. It's time we take our own advice and think strategically about how we approach our territories. If you're ahead of the game, you'll find more time to think strategically.

I want to give you a monthly timeline of how you should be thinking and approaching your sales territory. We're assuming you're on the calendar fiscal year (Jan 1 through December 31). We're also assuming you've been in the territory for nine months, or at least you're not brand new to the sales territory.

The Importance of Staying One Quarter Ahead of Your Peers

Always stay one quarter ahead of your peers when you think about strategic planning for the new year. You need to start developing your plan in September of the previous year if you want to get ahead. Set your revenue goal for the upcoming year, but most importantly, set the timeline for when you will accomplish that goal. Remember what I said about getting ahead and how that improves your quality of life? The timeline for when you achieve the goal is just as important as the goal itself. When you don't need the deal, more deals will come as a result.

Lastly, shoot for double your annual quota, or estimate what that might look like based on historical quota information. If you need some motivation, calculate how much commission you'll receive by making 200 percent of your quota and how you'll invest or spend that money.

As an example, my typical annual quota is $1 million. My goal is to achieve this number by June, or the end of Q2. Also, I want to finish the fiscal year at $2 million, or 200 percent of my annual plan.

Now break that goal down by quarter: $2 million / 4 quarters = $500,000 per quarter. My average deal size is $100,000, and $500,000 / $100,000 average size deal = 5 deals per quarter. Based on my discovery-to-close ratio of 3:1 last year, I need about fifteen deals in my pipeline at an average of $100,000 per deal to stay on track for this goal.

This is basic pipeline management for sales professionals. The real value of this exercise is giving yourself the motivational gut check. Is your pipeline short? Yes? Well then, it's time to ramp up your activity and drive new pipeline.

For motivational purposes, calculate your projected gross income for achieving 200 percent of your plan. Most technology companies will have an accelerator rate after you achieve your quota. This means your commission rate will increase from 100 to 200 percent of plan. Based on my research and assuming you have an enterprise software sales job, your yearly gross income (including base salary) should be anywhere from $250,000 to $600,000 for achieving 200 percent of your annual plan. And that, my friends, is a lot of cheddar.

Now think about what you plan to do with that money and how it's going to positively impact your life. Whatever you're going to do with the money, write it down, and then print it out. Then put that piece of paper right next to your desk or somewhere where you'll see it every single day.

This exercise is going to keep you motivated throughout the course of the year. We discussed fueling your resiliency fire; this is another way to keep that fire burning.

By now we know what we want to accomplish and our timeline for achieving our next year's goals. The next step in the process is a data-scrub refresh. We discussed the importance of data scrubbing earlier, as it's the foundation for our success. Now would be a good time to refresh your lists and ensure you have your eyes set on the right targets. If you skip this, you're hurting yourself. People change jobs all the time; we must ensure we're keeping an eye on these changes and, at a minimum updating our territory contacts once a quarter.

October—Your focus is closing out your current deals in play and building a massive pipeline going into Q1. Since you've been in the role for nine months, your first October campaign is going to be reaching out to all the people who have said no. You want to give them a compelling reason to revisit your proposal and start stacking meetings for the month of January. Stacking meetings for the first two weeks in January will help you get off to a fast start. Again, I'm going to drill home that getting ahead of the game will improve your quality of life.

Action Plan—Assume you're on the calendar fiscal year (Jan 1 through December 31):

1. Set your new-year goals, quarterly goals, and timelines for achieving those goals in September.

2. Calculate how much money you'll make by achieving 200 percent of plan. Then write down how that money will positively impact your life. Use this as a motivation to build the pipeline.

3. Revisit old sale cycles and start stacking meetings for the first two weeks in January to ensure a fast start.

4. Most importantly, getting ahead and staying ahead will improve your quality of life.

CHAPTER 8

The Agile Sales Professional—How to Evolve with Your Sales Territory

Nobody wants to be a one-hit wonder; you want to be successful year over year. With YOY success come YOY pay increases. Trust me; once you see your first large end-of-year commission check, you'll be hooked. We've discussed a consistent process and sales approach to ensure YOY success. Now it's time to talk about being agile and evolving with your sales territory.

Let's first define agile. Agile—the first definition states, "the ability to move quickly and easily." The second definition states, "the ability to frequently reassess and readapt to your environment." To me, agile sales professionals are a combination of both definitions. They're able to move quickly but are strategic enough to evolve their strategy based on their territory market opportunity.

What worked for you twenty-four months ago might not work for you in the future. As your technology company scales its business, your sales territory will probably shrink over time. Now, we can be like 80 percent of sales reps and freak out about the territory cuts, or we can be the agile sales professional who finds a way to adapt quickly to a new environment.

Before you start prospecting in a modified sales territory, you want to take a strategic approach to truly accessing your market's opportunity. If you have a hundred accounts to go after, your strategy should be different than it would be if you had ten accounts to go after. The rule of thumb is that you'll have to become more personalized over time to get meetings. If you have a ton of accounts to go after, you can probably get away with mail merges only. However, as you start having success, those opportunities will begin to shrink, and you'll need to adapt.

When you start in a new sales territory, think about how long you want to stay in that role based on the available market opportunity. Let me give you an example. If you have thirty accounts to go after, you want to be strategic and sell larger deals. If you have two hundred accounts, you can probably afford to be more transitional and sell smaller deals to be successful. In the world of technology sales, change is going to happen every single year. It might be acquisitions, new products, territory cuts, and so on. The key here is staying strategic and adapting to your new environment.

There is also a bit of a mind-set issue you'll need to deal with. In 2013, I sold $1 million in a territory that had a historical performance of $300,000 annually. My reward was my commissions, and they decided to cut my territory in half the following year. Also, my quota stayed the same. This meant less opportunity with the same quota liability.

I'll admit, I was livid. And at that time in my career, being agile was a new concept to me. Can you blame me? I had just sold $1 million and made a ton of money. Why would I want anything to change? As I became wiser, I realized it wasn't anything personal.

It's how the model works when you sell for a publicly traded company. There are only fifty states in America, and the business needs to have constant growth YOY for the shareholders. Therefore, you can grow through account expansion, bring new products to market, and increase your sales force to penetrate more market opportunity. When you increase your sales force, each of those people will need a sales territory. And since there are only fifty states, it has to come from somewhere.

When this happened, I thought, how the hell am I going to make this work? Sound familiar? As time went on, I adjusted my approach. I realized if I was going to achieve the same kind of success, I needed to change my mind-set and adapt to my new environment.

The first thing I did was a refresh data scrub of the territory. With half the accounts to go after, I needed to add more contacts to my database for each of the accounts I had. The year prior, I had about three contacts per account. I doubled it to six contacts to improve my odds of getting a discovery meeting.

I then spent more time truly understanding where my best opportunities were. As you can imagine, discovery meetings are harder to get with half the territory. So I evolved. I became more personalized with everyone and started adding value in every interaction. I stopped asking all the time and started giving value all the time. I also knew it was time to stop being transactional and start thinking strategically about my long-term success. This meant selling larger-size deals. In my world, when I sell an account, it goes to an account-management team, as they're better fitted for servicing our clients. This means that once I sell an account, I lose the ability to ever sell to them again.

Selling larger-size deals was purely a mind-set issue for me. I had sold a ton of $32,000 deals in the past, but I knew it wasn't going to work in the future. Closing my first $100,000-plus deal was a real eye-opener. I learned three critical lessons as a result of my first $100,000 deal: (1) $100,000 or $1 million is completely a mind-set issue, (2) selling bigger deals is better for the client, as they get more value out of the service, and the retention rates are higher with bigger-size deals, and (3) the sales-cycle time on the $32,000 deal and the $100,000-plus deal are the same. In my experience, the smaller the deal, the more challenging the customers will be.

As I mentioned, I had sold $1 million the year prior with double the territory. The next year I sold $950,000 with half the territory. To this day, I am grateful for the territory cuts. As a result of this cut, my skills evolved, and I became tighter with every prospect interaction.

In technology sales, the only consistency is change. Every single year, you're going to experience change. The first step is getting your mind right by knowing you can evolve and sustain success YOY. Second, what you did last year might not work for you this year. Become agile and adapt to your new environment. Reevaluate your territory market opportunity, rescrub your market by adding new contacts, and, finally, sell bigger deals.

CHAPTER 9

Picking the Right Technology Company to Maximize Your Earnings

Picking the right technology company to work for will have a huge impact on your potential earnings. There are thousands of different technologies on the market. Not all are created equal. You can be the greatest sales professional in the world, but if you have a product that you're not confident in, then you will not be successful.

If you're new to technology sales, you want to pick an organization you can grow with. If you're a tenured technology sales professional, you have the luxury of being more selective. In this book, we've discussed a sales process that will help you make incredible money. A proven, repeatable sales process is only part of the equation for making a ton of money in technology sales. The company you choose to work for will play a huge role as well.

At the time of this writing, Gartner covers over seven hundred different types of technologies. They even have a free IT glossary to help you understand each market segment.

With so many options, where do you begin? Those of you who have been around know there is no way to eliminate risk when starting a new job. You can conduct all the research in the world, but there are things you won't be able to figure out until you're on the inside. However, there are some things we can do to improve our probability of working for a great company in a hot market.

Most people will start by picking the company and seeing if they have any job openings. While the overall company is important, I recommend you start by picking a technology market and then find a company that is well positioned within that technology market. Let's use Salesforce, for example; they have very strong brand equity. They're the clear leader in the CRM market. However, just because they're the leader in the CRM market doesn't mean they're the leader in other market segments. Most technology companies have multiple streams of product revenues, so be sure you understand what product you'll be responsible for selling. You want to do your research on the market that product serves to understand the opportunity. Don't get blindsided just because the company has a powerful brand. Not all their offerings will be created equal.

How to Predict Employer and Technology Market Opportunity

The challenge is that every single technology provider will tell you they're the leader in XYZ. Well, if everyone is the leader, where do you start in regards to finding the right opportunity?

Step one. Google "Enterprise IT spending." You'll find several articles on IT spending forecasts. I found credible research that states enterprise security spending will grow by 8 percent to $96.3 billion in 2018. That's a massive market that I would love to get my hands on.

Step Two. Based on your research, you understand that enterprises will be investing heavily in cloud security technologies. Now what? There are thousands of different enterprise security technologies out there (we're not looking at companies yet).

Gartner creates reports called Hype Cycles. This report offers several benefits, and at the time of this writing, they have published about 111 Hype Cycles. Each represents a different market segment.

In the Gartner Hype Cycle report for cloud security, there are roughly thirty-two different categories of cloud security technologies. There are two things you want to know. Of these thirty-two different technologies, which will be a big deal, and when will they be highly adopted?

Many enterprises are risk adverse. You might have heard the term; no CIO ever got fired for selecting Microsoft, Oracle, or SAP. From a sales standpoint, this means you could have the greatest technology in the world, but many large enterprises will want to see it highly adopted before they buy. Or, in other words, many prefer to make safe investments in technology.

In the Hype Cycle, there is a section called "Technology Priority Matrix." It will rate the thirty-two different categories of cloud security technologies. It will rate them by benefit level—low, moderate, high, and transformational. Also, it will predict the number of years until mainstream adoption.

If you're in tech sales, you have a much greater shot at making a ton of money if you're selling a highly beneficial technology. Common sense, right? You want to be selling a technology that will have the greatest impact on the business. The other part of the equation is years to mainstream adoption, which in this report can be less than two years to more than ten years out.

Mainstream Adoption—Don't Be Too Early or Too Late

Back to my statement that "No CIO ever got fired for buying Oracle, SAP, or Microsoft." If your technology segment is not predicted to be mainstream adopted for ten years, it might be a real challenge to sell it. On the other side, if it's less than two years, you might be late to the party, meaning the companies that sell that offering probably have a pretty mature sales force who have been doing this for a while. This can make quota higher and territories smaller (not always), which is not good for your checking account. The perfect adoption period seems to be around two to five years.

For example, Gartner's Hype Cycle report for cloud security is telling you that cloud access security is a highly beneficial technology that will be mainstream adopted in the next two to five years. Two to five years is perfect because you're not too early or too late to the party.

Before we discuss selecting the right technology company, let's recap how you determined that cloud access security was a potential space you wanted to get into.

1. You Googled "Enterprise IT Spending" and found that enterprise security is predicted to grow by 8 percent to $96.3 billion (growth is good!).
2. You researched Gartner's Hype Cycle for cloud security—you paid for it.
3. You found out that of the thirty-two different technologies in cloud security, cloud access security brokers will be a highly beneficial technology that will be mainstream adopted in the next two to five years via the section in the report called "Technology Priority Matrix."

A best practice: If you have experience in X industry or X technology, start by researching those segments. For example, if you're an insurance broker and want to get into tech, there is a massive amount of technology spending from insurance companies. Try to pick a market that complements what you already know or what you're already passionate about.

The Power of Brand Equity

Based on your research, you've determined there could be massive earning potential in the cloud access security brokers space. Your next step is to Google "magic quadrant for cloud access security brokers." Odds are you'll find the document on a technology vendor's website.

This document is the same document many of your enterprise prospects will use in determining which vendor to buy from. The hardest part of any sale is getting the initial discovery meeting. If your prospect is in the market for this type of technology, being short-listed on this document will help you get in the door. On the other side, if the company is not on this document, it's going to be an uphill battle to win the deal.

In the top right-hand corner of this document, you'll see three vendors short-listed as leaders: Netskope, Symantec, and Skyhigh Networks. You now have a list of three technology companies you might want to work for.

This is just an example, but you could do this exercise for just about any viable technology market. Now I've boiled down my three potential employers. In summary, there will always be a certain level of risk when you start a new position at a new company. Use this process to help mitigate that risk and give yourself the best chance to make incredible money.

Size Matters—Income Potential at a Startup vs. a Large Technology Company
Why the Startup?

Startups can have a completely different feel than large corporations, from a culture standpoint. This book is about making incredible money in technology sales. Therefore, we're going to explore the pros and cons from a financial standpoint versus the cultural standpoint. Startups typically have one of two end goals in mind: to get acquired by a larger organization or to grow all the way up to IPO (initial public offering), meaning they become publicly traded. The reason most sales professionals will work at a startup is that they will get a very small percentage of equity or ownership in the company. Even a fraction of a percent can mean big bucks if the company gets acquired or makes it to IPO. If we're looking at the pros and cons from the financial aspects, I would say the percentage of equity is the biggest pro for working at a startup.

The second pro that comes to mind is that it could be a quick way to skyrocket to the top of the corporate ladder if you get in on the ground floor. However, you want to make sure you understand the company's exit strategy. For example, many companies' goal is to get acquired, get paid, and ride away into the sunset. If the goal is to get acquired by a large organization, there is a good chance you'll become just another employee of a larger company or, potentially, lose your job as a result of overlap after the acquisition. Again, these risks are justified if you have a piece of equity at the organization.

Sweet Spot Startup

I sold to CEOs and CMOs at startups in a previous role. It was a great experience getting to interact with these executives; often, if I did my job correctly, I would get the sale and a job offer from the person I had just sold to. With three kids, I was always too risk adverse to join a ground-floor startup—say, fewer than twenty-five employees. If I didn't have kids, it might have been a different story.

I've worked with hundreds of emerging technology companies. From these interactions, I did notice there was a sweet spot from a sales perspective—meaning, from a sales earnings standpoint, you don't want to be too early to join or too late to the party. That sweet spot seems to be around $15 million to $250 million in annual revenue.

Why $15 million to $250 million in revenue? When a product or company reaches $15 million in annual revenue, they're no longer a risky purchase for a CIO. Also, they start building a bit of brand equity, which can help you get more discovery meetings. Most importantly, they have a ton of market opportunity left to capture with very reasonable growth quotas. I remember speaking to a CEO who told me his top 20 percent of reps were making over $1 million per year. The other benefit here is that you should have a decent amount of run rate within your territory. Therefore, you can stay in the same role for a longer period and make great money. It will probably be a challenge for you to get equity if you join the company too late, but never say never. You can always ask.

Best Practice: Most of these companies are still private, which means the revenue data is harder to find. Inc.com publishes the Inc 5000 list (click here) every year. This is a list of high-growth companies by industry. There is a ton of value in this free list. Primarily, they'll list software companies' YOY growth rate, metro area, and revenue. Use this list as part of your research process to identify potential targets. Moreover, remember this: a growing company is a happy company, which will create more opportunities for career advancement and income.

Cons of a Startup

Often, startups cannot pay you as much money as large software companies (not always). Yet I would work at a startup if I truly believed in it, and if my compensation included equity in the company. You're going to have to do more with fewer resources. Your products might not be fully baked out, and you're only as good as your product offering. The number-one challenge you'll have to overcome is getting a discovery meeting with a CIO who has never heard of your company, meaning you have no brand equity. For my risk tolerance, I believe the $50 million revenue benchmark is best for my solution. Again, there is no one size fits all. Certain people can stomach more risk than others.

Large Software Company (Pros vs. Cons)

Large organizations have much more resources for marketing, product development, human resources, and so on. The biggest benefit is typically the nonmonetary benefits such as 401K, PTO, health care, and so on. Moreover, the compensation can be higher. The hardest part of any sales cycle is getting the initial meeting. The biggest benefit from a sales standpoint is going to be how much positive brand equity the company has. Also, many large organizations will have dozens of different products, which can create more opportunities for you.

One of the biggest challenges is that at times there can be too many cooks in the kitchen—some organizations will align territories by product offering. If the features of the products overlap, you could find yourself competing against your own company, meaning two reps are selling to the same CIO. This is never a good place to be.

My recommendation: If you're new, start with an organization that has a well-built-out or mature sales process. Get yourself established with a recognizable brand. Then, after you gain some experience, you can work your way up or jump to a startup for some equity.

CHAPTER 10

Putting It All Together

We've come a long way since page 1. We've covered a ton of tactics to ensure your long-term success. Technology sales is hard, but I truly believe it can be one of the most rewarding professions in the world. You get the opportunity to work with brilliant C-level executives every single day. Technology products have zero carbon footprint on the environment. Often, you'll have the ability to work from home. Also, if you play your cards right, you can become a multimillionaire by working as an individual contributor sales professional.

If you think about it, there are only two core components to making incredible money in technology sales. Those two core components are generating more pipeline and closing more pipeline. That's it. Everything we've been discussing is designed to help you with those two components.

Regarding the first component of generating more pipeline, we've discussed how to stay motivated by fueling your resiliency fire. We've discussed a core system of automation for driving new pipeline. We've discussed the details of journey-mapping execution and leveraging digital tools in the digital era.

Regarding the second component of closing more pipeline, we've mastered the discovery meeting, and we know how to create internal champions via personal value. We've discussed closing the sale with justification statements and how to stay top of mind between interactions.

Also, I hope you received value in between those two core components. We discussed strategies to ensure your long-term success, such as how to get ahead and stay ahead of your peers. We've discussed the importance of becoming an agile sales professional and adapting to your new environment. Lastly, we discussed how to understand what to look for when picking the right technology employer.

I hope that this book helps you make more money for yourself and for your family and that it gives you more capital to do good deeds in your local community. My commitment to you is the same as it was at the very beginning of this book. I promise that if you implement these processes, you will save yourself time and increase your sales. If you're trying to break into technology sales, discuss these processes during the interview, and you will land a job at the right technology company.

If you've made it this far reading this book, you're officially ready to make incredible money in technology $ales! Thank you for reading, and happy hunting!

Sincerely,
Mike Slattery
Author—*How to Make Incredible Money in Technology $ales*
Mike@professional-brand.com
Connect with me on Linked-In